M3 MACBOOK AIR

USER MANUAL

The Beginners and Seniors Guide to Master the 13-Inch & 15-Inch MacBook Air with M3 Chip for macOS Sonoma

BY

JOHNSON SMITH

TABLE OF CONTENTS

4

CHAPTER ONE

INTRODUCING M3 MACBOOK AIR

THE BEST AI CONSUMER LAPTOP IN THE WORLD

With the adoption of Apple silicon, each Mac is now an ideal AI platform. A speedier and more efficient 16-core Neural Engine, accelerators in the CPU and GPU to enhance on-device machine learning, and M3 make the MacBook Air the finest consumer laptop for artificial intelligence in the world. By capitalizing on this extraordinary AI performance, macOS provides users with intelligent features that amplify productivity and ingenuity. For instance, they can activate robust camera functionalities, real-time speech-to-text translation, text predictions, visual comprehension, accessibility features, and numerous others.

The displays of two new 13- and 15-inch MacBook Airs with M3 processor

Users have access to an extensive ecosystem of applications that provide sophisticated AI functionalities. For instance, Goodnotes 6 offers AI Math Assistance for assignment verification, Pixelmator Pro automatically enhances photographs, and CapCut eliminates background noise from videos. In conjunction with the unified memory architecture of Apple silicon, the MacBook Air is capable of executing locally optimized AI models with exceptional performance, such as large language models (LLMs) and diffusion models for image generation. MacBook Air supports cloud-based solutions in addition to on-device performance, allowing users to run AI-powered productivity and creative applications such as Canva, Adobe Firefly, Microsoft Copilot for Microsoft 365, and Microsoft Copilot.

EVERYONE'S FAVORITE

MacBook Air is the preferred laptop among a greater number of people, and the M3 further elevates the standard with its extraordinary blend of performance, portability, and user-prized features.

THE DESIGN

The MacBook Air 13- and 15-inch models feature an aluminum enclosure that is designed to endure heavy usage. Additionally, these devices are exceptionally lightweight and less than half an inch thin, allowing users to conveniently carry out tasks such as work, play, or creation. The 13-inch model offers increased screen real estate for multitasking, whereas the 15-inch model provides the utmost portability. Students who are constantly on the move and business professionals who prefer a larger screen can both find the ideal dimension.

EXCELLENT LIQUID RETINA DISPLAY

The MacBook Air showcases an exquisite Liquid Retina display, which is available in 13.6- or 15.3-inch sizes. This display supports 1 billion colors, has a maximum luminosity of 500 nits, and has a resolution that is up to two times that of comparable PC laptops. The content exhibits vividness and precise details, while the text demonstrates exceptional clarity.

TWO EXTERNAL DISPLAYS SUPPORTED

MacBook Air with M3 now can accommodate a maximum of two external displays when the laptop lid is closed. This feature is particularly advantageous for business users or individuals who necessitate multiple displays to perform tasks such as document distribution or app multitasking simultaneously.

A user utilizes the two external displays of the new MacBook Air to complete some work. The 13-inch MacBook Air is offered in two ideal versions, with the 15-inch model providing an additional 15 inches of screen space for multitasking in a slender and lightweight construction.

VERSATILE WITH CONNECTION

The Wi-Fi 6E standard on the MacBook Air with M3 enables download speeds that are up to two times faster than the previous generation. In addition, a 3.5mm headphone input and two Thunderbolt interfaces for connecting accessories are included, as is MagSafe charging.

CAMERA, MICROPHONES, AND SPEAKERS

Users can maintain an optimal appearance while engaging in FaceTime HD conversations with loved ones or conducting global business collaborations by utilizing a 1080p camera. In addition, a three-microphone array and enhanced voice clarity for audio and video conversations will allow users to sound their finest. The MacBook Air is equipped with an immersive sound system that incorporates Dolby Atmos and Spatial Audio, allowing users to experience movies and music in three-dimensional soundstages.

TOUCH ID AND MAGIC KEYBOARD

The full-height function row on the comfortable and silent backlit Magic Keyboard enables users to unlock their Mac, sign in to apps and websites, and make purchases with Apple Pay with a single fingerstroke securely and conveniently.

At midnight, an up-close shot of the keyboard of the brand-new MacBook Air.

A vibrant red furry garment is displayed on the new MacBook Air, adorning the user.

When combined with macOS, the MacBook Air offers an unparalleled experience:

macOS Sonoma: MacBook Air now supports the placement of widgets directly on the desktop, one-click interaction with them, and access to an extensive ecosystem of iPhone widgets. Enhanced video conferencing is facilitated by noteworthy functionalities such as Presenter Overlay and Reactions. Safari's profiles maintain navigational separation across multiple projects or topics, whereas web applications expedite access to preferred websites. Moreover, Game Mode enhances the gaming experience.

A rise in productivity: With the assistance of Split View, all users, including business professionals, can maximize the expansive display on the MacBook Air or spread out across multiple screens by connecting up to two external displays. Additionally, functions such as Stage Manager assist users, such as students, in concentrating on the current task.

Enhanced by iPhone: Continuity enables the MacBook Air to operate without interruption on the iPhone and other Apple devices. Users can share and receive documents, photographs, and more via AirDrop and other similar functionalities on neighboring Apple devices. The Universal Clipboard enables users to copy and paste text, images, or videos from one application on one Apple device to another application on a nearby Mac with ease. The Continuity Camera feature enables users to effortlessly capture or scan adjacent objects using their iPhone and have them instantaneously displayed on their Mac. Handoff enables users to initiate a task on one Apple device, such as responding to an email, and effortlessly complete it on another.

Vast selection of apps: MacBook Air includes productivity applications such as Pages, Numbers, and Keynote, in addition to FaceTime, Freeform, iMovie, GarageBand, and Photos, which enable users to effortlessly produce exceptional work. Moreover, thousands of apps have been optimized for Apple hardware, allowing users' preferred applications, such as Microsoft 365 and numerous iOS apps, to operate at an exceptionally rapid speed on macOS.

CHAPTER TWO

DETAILED EXPLORATION OF THE FEATURES

The 13-inch as well as 15-inch MacBook Air models recently released are equipped with M3 chips. They have the features enumerated below:

A left-side perspective of a MacBook Air, emphasizing the Thunderbolt/USB 4 and MagSafe 3 connectors.

❖ **Thunderbolt / USB 4 ports:** Connect to a display or projector, transfer data at Thunderbolt 3 or USB 4 speeds (up to 40 Gbit/s), as well as charge your computer. Additionally, gadgets like an iPad, rechargeable trackpad, or keyboard can be charged through the sockets.

An animation depicting the power adapter cable being inserted into the MacBook Air receptacle.

❖ **MagSafe port:** Utilize the USB-C power adapter that is included to recharge the battery of the

MacBook Air. When the battery requires recharging, the indicator light illuminates amber; it turns green once the battery is completely charged. The optional 70W USB-C Power Adapter can elevate the battery life of your MacBook Air with an M3 chip to 50 percent in approximately 30 minutes.

A view from the right side of a MacBook Air, emphasizing the 3.5 mm headphone port.

❖ **3.5 mm port for headphones:** Utilize external speakers or stereo headphones to stream your preferred music or films. Even high-impedance headphones can be utilized without an amplifier or digital-to-analog converter.

A top-down view of an unobstructed MacBook Air, emphasizing the Force Touch trackpad, FaceTime HD camera, microphones, as well as Touch ID (power button).

- ❖ **Speakers**: A six-speaker sound system comprises two tweeters as well as two sets of force-cancelling woofers for the 15-inch MacBook Air with an M3 processor. Two tweeters as well as two woofers comprise the four-speaker sound system of the 13-inch MacBook Air using an M3 processor. With both, Dolby Atmos provides support for music and movies, allowing for an immersive audio experience that incorporates spatial audio.
- ❖ **FaceTime HD 1080p camera:** Engage in FaceTime video conversations while capturing video and images. The camera system produces video of exceptional quality and performs admirably in low light. A green indicator light situated adjacent to the camera signifies that it is operational.
- ❖ **Touch ID**: To power on the MacBook Air, select Touch ID (also the power button), or simply raise the lid. Additionally, you can secure your Mac using the Touch ID icon. Upon initial system startup or restore a password entry prompt will appear. You can utilize Touch ID for Apple Pay purchases as well as authenticate with a touch rather than entering your password after your initial registration, once Touch ID is configured.
- ❖ **Force touch trackpad**: Utilize trackpad gestures to operate your MacBook Air with Force Touch. By utilizing the entire trackpad surface as a trigger, it is effortless to touch anywhere.

❖ **Microphones:** The three-microphone array is integrated for communicating with peers or recording audio.

THE COMPONENTS THAT COMPRISE YOUR MACBOOK AIR

The MacBook Air comes with two accessories, a cable and one of the power adapters specified below, which are required for operation.

The accessory	The Description
AC plug	**30W USB-C Power Adapter:** Compatible with 13-inch MacBook Airs with M3 chips and MacBook Airs with M2 chips. After connecting the power adapter, extend the electrical prongs on the AC connector to their maximum extent and insert the adapter into an AC power receptacle.
AC plug	**Compact power adapter using dual 35W USB-C ports:** For 13- as well as 15-inch MacBook Air models with M3 chips. After connecting the power adapter, stretch the electrical prongs on the AC connector to their maximum extent as well as insert the adapter into an AC power receptacle.
AC plug	**67W USB-C Power Adapter or 70W USB-C Power Adapter:** Not required for MacBook Air 13-inch and 15-inch models with the M3 CPU. After connecting the power adapter, lengthen the electrical prongs on the AC connector to their

maximum extent and insert the adapter into an AC power receptacle. The 70W USB-C Power Adapter enables rapid charging of the MacBook Air featuring the M3 chip, achieving a 50% charge in approximately 30 minutes.

MAGIC KEYBOARD FOR MACBOOK AIR

Utilizing the built-in functions of the Magic Keyboard using Touch ID, it is effortless to input emojis, alter keyboard languages, secure your MacBook Air, as well as execute numerous system functions. By configuring Touch ID, users will be able to utilize their fingerprints to unlock the MacBook Air, swiftly secure the screen, and complete transactions using Apple Pay on websites, the App Store, the Apple TV app, as well as Apple Books.

Configure Touch ID. Touch ID can be configured during setup or later in the Touch ID & Password section of System Settings.

Activate the MacBook Air. Alternatively, you may raise the faceplate, select Touch ID (the power button), or any other key.

Employ Touch ID. When you resume or power on your computer after configuring Touch ID, you will be prompted to enter your password. Following the initial authentication process, in subsequent password inquiries within the same session, you may securely validate by gently touching the Touch ID sensor with your finger. Touch ID can also be used to make secure online purchases with Apple Pay.

Secure the MacBook Air. Touch ID enables you to secure your screen rapidly.

Deactivate the MacBook Air. To disable your MacBook Air, select Shut Down from the Apple menu . To enter slumber mode on your MacBook Air, select Apple > slumber from the menu.

Implement function controls. These common system features are accessible via shortcuts located on the function keys in the upper row:

- **luminosity Adjustment (F1, F2):** To modify the screen's luminosity, utilize the Decrease brightness or Increase brightness keys, respectively.
- **Mission Control (F3):** To observe the current state of your MacBook Air, which includes all open windows as well as spaces, select the Mission Control key.
- **Spotlight Search (F4):** To initiate Spotlight and conduct a search on your MacBook Air, select the Spotlight key.
- **Dictation and Siri (F5):** To enable dictation, press the Microphone key. This feature allows you to dictate text in any application that supports typing, including Messages, Mail, Pages, and

others. Click and hold the Microphone key🎤 for Siri to become operational, then utter your request immediately.

❖ To enable or disable Do Not Disturb, select the Do Not Disturb icon☾ (F6). You will not be able to see or hear notifications on MacBook Air when Do Not Disturb is enabled; however, you can access them later via Notification Centre.

❖ **Media (F7, F8, F9):** To fast-forward a song, movie, or slideshow, click the Fast-forward key ▷▷; to retrace ◁◁, press the Play/halt key▷||; or to play or halt, click the Fast-forward key.

❖ **Mute (F10):** To silence the internal speakers or the 3.5 mm headphone port, select the Mute key◁.

❖ The volume can be adjusted by pressing the Decrease volume key◁⁾ or the Increase volume key◁⁾⁾⁾ through the Bluetooth audio gadget, built-in speakers, or 3.5 mm headphone port (F11, F12).

Function keys might perform alternative functions or execute actions within specific applications; for instance, the F11 key can conceal all active windows as well as reveal the desktop. While pressing a function key, strike as well as hold the Function (Fn)/Globe key🌐 to activate the alternative feature associated with that key.

Modify the keypad configuration. To configure the Function (Fn)/Globe key⊕ as well as keypad options, navigate to System Preferences and select Keyboard from the sidebar. Altering the luminance as well as illumination of the keyboard, determining whether the Function (Fn)/Globe key⊕ launches dictation, modifies the input source, or displays the emoji picker/Character Viewer, as well as adjusting keyboard shortcuts are all possible.

Employ symbols as well as emoji. To access the emoji selection, hold down the Function (Fn)/Globe key⊕ (if enabled in the Keypad settings). Utilize the emoji selector to search for or browse through emoji by category, as well as to insert icons such as pictographs.

Gain knowledge of keypad shortcuts. You can execute specific operations on the MacBook Air more rapidly by pressing key combinations, as well as perform operations that you would typically execute using a trackpad or mouse. To copy selected text, for instance, select Command-C after which click the location where you wish to paste the text before pressing Command-V.

MACBOOK AIR TRACKPAD

Simple trackpad gestures enable you to perform a variety of tasks on your MacBook Air, including navigating through webpages, zooming in or documents, and rotating photographs. The Force Touch trackpad enhances interactivity with the addition of pressure-sensing capabilities. The trackpad offers feedback in the form of a subtle vibration that indicates the alignment of objects when they are rotated or dragged, enabling more precise work.

The following are frequent gestures:

Gesture	Action
	Click by pressing any location on the trackpad. Alternatively, enable "Tap to click" in the Trackpad Settings and tap.
	To force a click, click followed by a deeper press. You can access additional information via force click; for instance, by clicking an address or a term, you can view its definition, while a preview of the location can be opened in Maps.
	Secondary click (or right-click): To access auxiliary menus, use two fingers. When "Tap to click" is activated, use two digits to press. Click the trackpad while holding down the Control key on the keyboard.
	Use two fingertips to navigate by gliding them upwards or downwards.
	Open and close your thumb as well as your finger to adjust the magnification level of images and websites.
	Swipe for navigation: To navigate employing webpages, documents, as well as

	more, utilize two fingertips to swipe left or right, similar to turning a page within a book.
	Execute Launchpad: Launch applications rapidly using Launchpad. To activate an application, pinch it shut with four to five fingertips, then click on it.
	Swipe across applications: To navigate between full-screen applications, use three or four digits to swipe left or right.

Tailor your hand gestures. Under System Preferences, select Trackpad from the sidebar. You can do the following:

❖ More information about each gesture
❖ Adjust the click pressure to your liking.
❖ Consider the implementation of pressure-sensing functions.
❖ Regulation of the monitoring pace
❖ Personalize additional trackpad functions

Advice: If you discover that you are inadvertently performing force clicks, consider increasing the click pressure within the Trackpad Settings. Alternately, alter the default configuration for "Look up & data detectors" from "Force Click with one finger" to "Tap with three fingers."

CHARGE THE BATTERY

The battery in the MacBook Air undergoes recharging whenever it is powered on.

A MacBook Air is equipped with a power adapter.

Bring the battery to life. Apply power to your MacBook Air by utilizing the power adapter and cable that are included with the product.

Display battery life in the menu bar. Incorporate a battery icon into your menu bar to access Battery settings and view information about your battery rapidly. Select Control Centre from the System Preferences menu, then navigate to Battery on the right as well as select Show in Menu Bar. Additionally, the battery percentage can be displayed in the menu bar.

Modify the battery configuration. Alternate battery configurations can be modified in the System Settings.

❖ **Optimized Battery Charging:** By analyzing your daily charging routine, this function reduces battery degradation and extends its lifespan. It attempts to fully charge the battery before unplugging when it anticipates that you will be connected for a prolonged duration, delaying charging by 80%. Select Battery from the sidebar of System Settings, then select the information icon next to Battery Health to enable Optimized Battery Charging.

❖ In low power mode, energy consumption is reduced. This is a viable alternative for extended periods away from a power source, such as when traveling. Select Battery in the sidebar of System Settings, and then select an option from the Low Power Mode pop-up menu.

In the Battery Settings menu, select Options to modify additional advanced settings, such as while to wake for network access, prevent automatic napping, and minimize the display when using the device on battery power.

Connecting the power adapter. Utilize either the MagSafe 3 port with the USB-C to MagSafe 3 Cable linked to the power adapter or one of the Thunderbolt ports with a USB-C Charge Cable to charge the battery on a MacBook Air with an M3 chip. Utilize the power adapter-connected USB-C Charge Cable and one of the Thunderbolt connectors to charge the battery on the MacBook Air with the M2 CPU.

Fast charging the MacBook Air with M3 chip to 50 percent in approximately 30 minutes is possible using the USB-C to MagSafe 3 cable as well as the optional 70W USB-C power adapter.

Assess the charge of the battery. To determine the battery level or charging status, observe the icon located to the right of the menu bar labeled "battery status." Or, navigate to System Preferences and select Battery from the sidebar.

Charging   Charged

The battery's charging and charged status icons.

Battery history of utilization. Navigate to System Preferences and select Battery to view the battery's consumption for the previous twenty-four hours or ten days.

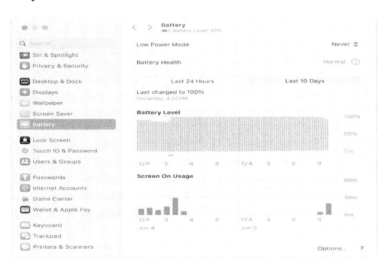

Battery Settings interface displaying energy consumption for the previous ten days. Additionally, the window displays the battery health as normal and provides the option to activate low-power mode.

Maintain battery life. You can increase the amount of time a given charge lasts a battery by decreasing the luminance of the display, closing unused applications, and disconnecting peripheral devices. To modify your power settings, select Battery from the sidebar of System Preferences. The battery of a connected device may deplete if the MacBook Air is in slumber mode at the time.

ACCESSORIES FOR THE MACBOOK AIR

Apple offers the subsequent adapters for connecting the MacBook Air to external displays, power sources, as well as gadgets, among other things.

Adapter or Cable	An exposition
	Using a USB-C to USB adapter, you can link the MacBook Air to conventional USB peripherals.
	Link the iPhone or other iOS or iPadOS gadget to the MacBook Air via a USB-C to Lightning cable to charge and sync.
	Utilizing the USB-C Digital AV Multiport Adapter, establish a connection between your MacBook Air and an HDMI display. Additionally, charge your device by connecting a USB-C charge cable and a standard USB device.

	Utilize the USB-C VGA Multiport Adapter to establish a connection between your MacBook Air and a VGA projector or display. Additionally, link a USB-C charge cable as well as a standard USB device to charge the MacBook Air.
	Adapter from Thunderbolt 3 (USB-C) to Thunderbolt 2: Use Thunderbolt 2 to link the MacBook Air to other devices.

IMPLEMENT ACCESSORIES USING A MACBOOK AIR

In addition to docking stations, the MacBook Air is compatible with a variety of peripherals, including mouse, trackpads, as well as wearable devices such as AirPods. Linking accessories to the MacBook Air is possible via Bluetooth technology or by linking a cable from the accessory to a single Thunderbolt/USB 4 interface.

Before embarking. Perform the following steps before connecting an accessory to the MacBook Air:

❖ Refer to the accompanying documentation for your accessory.
❖ When establishing a connection via cable, ensure that you are using the appropriate cable. To link the cable to the Thunderbolt/USB 4 port on the MacBook Air, an adapter may be required as well.
❖ The macOS operating system on your MacBook Air should be up-to-date.

Link A Wireless Accessory Together

Activate Bluetooth. Select the icon⬚ for the Control Centre from the menu bar. When Bluetooth is activated, the indicator changes to blue. Click the icon⬚ when it is grey to activate Bluetooth.

Configure a Bluetooth device. Pairing a Bluetooth accessory with the MacBook Air is required the first time you use it. For information on how to activate Bluetooth, consult the manual that accompanies the accessory. For instance, to ensure that it is ready to connect, you may need to toggle a switch on the accessory. Both the Mac as well as the accessory must be nearby and powered on.

Launch the Bluetooth application in the sidebar of System Preferences on your Mac when the accessory is prepared to connect. After selecting the accessory from the list of Nearby Devices, click Connect.

A Bluetooth accessory is linked. Once an accessory has been connected, it will communicate to your MacBook Air automatically. To determine which Bluetooth devices have been linked to your MacBook Air, click the Control Centre icon⬚ in the menu bar, then hover over Bluetooth and select the corresponding arrow. Accessories that possess a blue icon in the inventory are interconnected.

If your accessory is not connecting automatically, navigate to Bluetooth in the System Preferences menu on your Mac. Ensure that the accessory is listed in My Devices. If the accessory does not appear, proceed with the pairing instructions.

Neglect to reconnect a Bluetooth accessory. To detach a Bluetooth accessory from your Mac, navigate to System Preferences and select Bluetooth. Click Disconnect after hovering your mouse over the accessory in the My Devices list. To prevent your MacBook Air from connecting to a Bluetooth accessory automatically, select Forget This Device from the Information symbol next to the accessory.

A magic keyboard, trackpad, or mouse must be connected. Utilize the cable included with the Magic Mouse, Magic Trackpad, or Magic Keyboard to establish a connection between your MacBook Air and the accessory. Then, slide the accessory's switch to the on position so that the green light is illuminated. The accessory is subsequently paired with the Mac.

Once the accessory has been paired with the MacBook Air, the cable can be disconnected to enable wireless operation. When Bluetooth is enabled, your Magic Mouse, Magic Trackpad, or Magic Keyboard will communicate with your Mac automatically.

Connect the AirPods to the MacBook Air. Follow the instructions at associate AirPods with an Apple Device to associate and connect AirPods.

Connect An Accessory Together Using A Cable

Certain accessories are cable-compatible with the MacBook Air. Depending on the abilities of the cable as well as the accessory, it may be possible to transmit data or charge the accessory while it is linked.

Be sure to refer to the accompanying documentation of the accessory before establishing a connection. Certain accessories require an additional power source to be connected via an electrical outlet.

You must use a cable that is compatible with both the port on the accessory and the Thunderbolt/USB 4 interface on your MacBook Air to connect an accessory. If the cable lacks the appropriate connector for the Mac, an adapter may be utilized to establish a connection.

Note: Certain accessories require initial approval; for more information.

CONNECT A DISPLAY EXTERNAL TO YOUR MACBOOK AIR

The MacBook Air is compatible with external displays, including the Apple Studio Display, a projector, and a television. The MacBook Air's USB-C connectors are capable of supporting video output.

Before commencing, verify that you have the appropriate cable to connect your display and consult the documentation that accompanies your display.

You can specify the resolution and refresh rate (Hz) of a connected display. For optimal performance, when increasing the refresh rate of your display, you should choose a lower resolution. Display parameters can be modified via System Preferences to affect the display's refresh rate and resolution.

To obtain further information regarding the display types that are supported by your MacBook Air, consult the Technical Specifications. Navigate to Display Support in the Help > MacBook Air Specifications section of the System Preferences (you may need to scroll).

Display Connectivity For A Macbook Air
Integrate a single external display with a maximum resolution of 6K at 60 Hz via a USB-C port.

After ensuring that the display is plugged into an electrical outlet, link your devices using the appropriate cables and interfaces.

Which Cable Do I Require?
❖ **Connect a VGA display or projector:** Connect the display or projector to a Thunderbolt / USB 4 port on your MacBook Air using a USB-C VGA Multiport Adapter.
❖ **HDMI display or TV connection:** Connect the HDMI display or TV to a Thunderbolt / USB 4 port on your MacBook Air using a USB-C Digital AV Multiport Adapter.

❖ Link a USB-C display to your MacBook Air by connecting it to a Thunderbolt or USB 4 interface.

An adapter is required to connect a display. You may find it possible to utilize your display with an adapter (sold separately) if its connector does not match the port you intend to use. Apple Store locations and other resellers can be accessed for availability and further details. Consult the display's manual or contact the manufacturer to ensure that you are selecting the correct product.

Use AirPlay on an Apple TV. By connecting a TV to an Apple TV, it is possible to utilize AirPlay to display the display of your MacBook Air on your TV. For more information.

Reorganize and modify displays. Once an external display or projector has been connected, navigate to System Settings and select Displays from the sidebar to configure the arrangement of the displays, designate one as the primary display, and modify the resolution. To mirror your screen, select the mirror option from the "Use as" menu after clicking the display you wish to use as a mirror.

CHAPTER THREE

MACBOOK AIR SETUP

CONFIGURE THE MACBOOK AIR

During the setup process of your new MacBook Air, you can modify specific Mac settings, activate features such as Touch ID, and migrate data from another device. Additionally, if you have a Mac, iPad, or iPhone, you may be able to expedite the setup process for your new Mac by bypassing certain stages and utilizing your existing configurations.

"Hello" appears on the display of an operational MacBook Air.

During the Mac setup process, if further assistance is required, an Apple expert is available via chat, email, phone, or by scheduling an appointment at the Genius Bar.

The Setup Assistant guides you through configuring your Mac so that you can begin using it.

If you wish to be guided through each procedure stage, select a link from the list below.

CONFIGURE A MACBOOK AIR FOR NOVICE MAC USERS

This comprehensive tutorial outlines every stage of the installation procedure and is designed to be utilized in conjunction with Setup Assistant.

Option selection may necessitate scrolling through certain phases. To determine how to scroll on a Mac, simply move your two fingertips up and down the trackpad.

Before commencing,

❖ Keep your iPhone or iPad nearby during the setup process, as certain stages may necessitate verification on an additional device.

❖ During the configuration process, it is possible to transmit data from an external device, such as a Windows PC. If you wish to accomplish this, ensure that the computer from which you wish to transmit data is powered on and updated with the most recent software version.

❖ Installing Setup Assistant on your MacBook Air is straightforward and should not require an excessive amount of time. However, if you decide to migrate data, you should allocate more time.

Establish Your Region Or Country, Language, And Wi-Fi Connection

Select a language. This enables the Mac's default language. To modify the language at a later time, navigate to System Preferences, select Language & Region from the sidebar, and press Enter.

Input your region or country. This configures the format of temperature, dates, currencies, and more on your Mac. To modify your settings at a later time, navigate to System Preferences, select Language & Region from the sidebar's General section, and then click General.

A configuration assistant interface containing options for the user to identify their country or region.

Enable accessibility functions. Select Not Now to view accessibility choices for vision, motor, hearing, as well as cognitive abilities. To configure VoiceOver for your Mac, select the Escape key on your keyboard. Touch ID, located in the upper-right corner of the keyboard, can also be triple-clicked to access additional accessibility options.

Establish a Wi-Fi connection. Select your Wi-Fi network and, if prompted, input its password. Additionally, you may select Other Network Options and adhere to the on-screen guidance when utilizing Ethernet. When connecting the Ethernet cable to the USB-C port on the MacBook Air, an additional Ethernet adapter is required...

To modify the Wi-Fi network at a later time, access the System Settings menu, select Wi-Fi from the sidebar, and if prompted, input the network's password.

Information Transfer From A Different Computer

Your data, including contacts, accounts, and files, can be migrated from your Windows PC to your freshly purchased Mac. If you wish to transfer information from a different Mac. You have the option of transferring the data wirelessly or via Ethernet cable from your Windows PC to your MacBook Air.

A Setup Assistant display bearing the inscription "Migration Assistant." The option to transmit data from a Windows computer is selected via a checkbox.

Before embarking. Ensure the software on your Windows computer is up-to-date with the most recent version. Migration Assistant is then downloaded to your Windows computer.

Wireless data transfer. Both the new Mac and the Windows PC must be connected to the same Wi-Fi network. On the configuration interface, select your Windows PC and proceed with the instructions.

Data transfer is performed via Ethernet cable. Integrate your Windows PC and Mac directly through the use of an Ethernet cable. When connecting the cable to the USB-C port on the MacBook Air, you will need an Ethernet adapter, including the Belkin USB-C to Gigabit Ethernet Adapter. Whether the Ethernet cable is compatible with the terminals on your Windows PC may necessitate the use of an adapter.

Select your Windows PC on the setup interface and proceed with the instructions once they are connected.

Later, transfer the data. Additionally, you may opt not to transfer data at this time. Select Not Now within the Migration Assistant window if this is the case. After setup, transmit data by consulting the transmit your data to the latest MacBook Air guide.

CREATE AN APPLE ID AND LOG IN TO YOUR COMPUTER

Utilize your Apple ID to log in. Apple IDs are probable in your possession if you own another Apple gadget, such as an iPhone or iPad. Currently, if you do not have an Apple ID, you can sign up for one at no cost.

Email and password are the components of your Apple ID. It is the account that is utilized for all interactions with Apple, encompassing the App Store, Apple TV app, iCloud, as well as additional functionalities. Your Apple ID and username and password that are used to access your Mac computer account are not identical.

You should maintain a unique Apple ID and avoid sharing it with others.

Perform a single action from this screen:

❖ If you're using an Apple ID, enter the password and email address associated with your account. A verification code will be sent to your iPhone or iPad if you possess one. In the absence of an iPhone or iPad, a verification code is transmitted via text message to the phone number linked to your Apple ID. Should the verification code or text not be received, proceed by following the instructions displayed on-screen.

❖ In the absence of an Apple ID, select "Create new Apple ID."

❖ To retrieve an Apple ID or password that you have forgotten, select "Forgot Apple ID or password."

❖ Select Set Up Later if you do not wish to enroll in or create an Apple ID at this point. You can sign in using an Apple ID or generate a new Apple ID after setup. To do so, navigate to System Preferences and select "Sign in with the Apple ID" from the sidebar.

After logging in with an Apple ID, please review the following terms and conditions. To approve, proceed after checking the Agree option.

Establish a computer login. Create an account with a username and password, which will subsequently be utilized to authorize additional actions or access your MacBook Air. If you neglect the password for the computer account, you may include an optional indication. To modify the logon image for your account, click it and then select an alternative.

Create a Computer Account

Fill out the following information to create your computer account.

Full name: Ashley Rico

Account name: ashleyrico
This will be the name of your home folder.

Password:

Hint:

☑ Allow my Apple ID to reset this password

Back   Continue

A Setup Assistant interface containing the text "Create a Computer Account."

Note: Your computer account is distinct from your Apple ID; however, if you enable this option during registration, you can utilize your Apple ID to reset the password to activate your Mac if you ever forget it.

CONVERT IT TO YOUR NEW MAC

If you have previously configured a different gadget with iPadOS 15 or later or iOS 15 or later, a prompt for express setup, Make This Your New Mac, will appear. Unless you possess an iPhone or iPad equipped with the appropriate software version, this phase is omitted.

Make This Your New Mac allows you to bypass several setup procedures by utilizing the settings that are already recorded in your iCloud account. To maintain your current configuration, select Continue. The configuration procedure proceeds directly to Touch ID as well as Apple Pay.

To modify your new MacBook Air's settings, select Customize Settings and continue to the following step.

PERSONALIZE THE SECURITY AND PRIVACY SETTINGS OF YOUR MAC, ACTIVATE SCREEN TIME, AND ENABLE SIRI

With Location Services enabled. Apps such as Maps can be granted access to your Mac's location. To modify your Location Services options at a later time, navigate to System Preferences, select Privacy & Security from the sidebar, and finally select Location Services.

In the absence of Location Services enabled a screen appears for time zone selection.

Distribute analytics to Apple and its developers. Determine if diagnostics and data should be transmitted to Apple and if Apple should be permitted to share incident and usage data with developers. Open System Preferences, select Privacy & Security from the sidebar, then Analytics & Improvements (scroll down if necessary), and then select Options to modify these settings at a later time.

Configure Screen Time. Screen Time enables you to monitor your MacBook Air's daily and weekly usage, set app usage limits, manage children's screen time, and more. Click Continue to activate; otherwise, select Set Up Later. If you opt to configure Screen Time at a later time, navigate to System Preferences and select Screen Time from the sidebar.

Protect your information with FileVault. FileVault aids in the protection of your data. You have the option to enable FileVault for data protection and to have your iCloud account activate the disc if you neglect the password during setup.

Deactivate Siri and "Hey Siri." During setup, you can activate Siri and "Hey Siri" to enable spoken commands. Enable Ask Siri to configure Siri. To configure "Hey Siri," when prompted, utter a series of Siri commands. To enable Siri and "Hey Siri" at a later time, select the desired options from the Siri & Spotlight sidebar within System Settings.

Additionally, you may elect to share audio with Apple to enhance Siri during setup. It is possible to modify the decision to share audio at a later time. Select the desired options by navigating to System Preferences, selecting Privacy & Security from the sidebar, and then selecting Analytics & Improvements (scroll down if necessary).

TOUCH ID AND APPLE PAY
CONFIGURATION

Touch ID (the top-right icon on your keyboard) can be personalized with a fingerprint during setup. This fingerprint can then be used to enroll into certain third-party applications, authorize purchases with Apple Pay, and unlock your MacBook Air. To establish Touch ID, adhere to the on-screen prompts. To modify Touch ID settings at a later time or to add more fingerprints, access System Settings and select Touch ID & Password from the sidebar. To submit a fingerprint, follow the on-screen instructions after clicking the submit icon $+$.

Establish Apple Pay. You can add a debit, credit, or store card that can be used to make purchases with Touch ID by configuring Apple Pay entering the card information, and following the on-screen instructions. You may be required to verify the card you currently employ for media purchases.

To configure Apple Pay or subsequently add more cards, navigate to System Preferences and select Wallet and Apple Pay. Utilize the on-screen instructions to configure Apple Pay.

Please be advised that the eligibility of your card for use with Apple Pay is determined by the card issuer, who may request supplementary information from you to finalize the verification procedure. A multitude of debit and credit cards are compatible with Apple

Pay. For details regarding the current credit card issuers and Apple Pay availability, please refer to the Apple Support article titled "Apple Pay Participating Banks."

Configure The Desktop Appearance

Select your style. Choose between Light, Dark, or Auto to customize the appearance of your desktop. If you wish to modify a setting you made during installation at a later time, navigate to System Preferences, pick Appearance, and then select an option. Additionally, other appearance parameters can be modified, including the size of auxiliary icons and the color of the highlights.

Note: This stage is omitted if you opt for express configuration with Make This Your New Mac.

Setup Is Finished

The upgraded MacBook Air is now operational.

CONFIGURE YOUR MACBOOK AIR FOR EXISTING MAC USERS

This comprehensive tutorial outlines every stage of the installation procedure and is designed to be utilized in conjunction with Setup Assistant.

Before Commencing

❖ Keep close to your alternative Mac, iPhone, or iPad throughout the setup process, as certain stages may necessitate substantiation on an additional device.

❖ During the configuration process, it is possible to transfer data from an additional Mac. If you wish to accomplish this, ensure that the computer from which you wish to transmit data is powered on and updated with the most recent software version.

❖ Installing Setup Assistant on your MacBook Air is straightforward and should not require an excessive amount of time. However, if you decide to migrate data, you should allocate more time.

Establish Your Region Or Country, Language, And Wi-Fi Connection

Select a language. This enables the Mac's default language. To modify the language at a later time, navigate to System Preferences, select Language & Region from the sidebar, and press Enter.

Input your region or country. This configures the format of temperature, dates, currencies, and more on your Mac. To modify your settings at a later time, navigate to System Preferences, select Language & Region from the sidebar's General section, and then click General.

A configuration assistant interface containing options for the user to identify their country or region.

Enable accessibility functions. Click Not Now to view accessibility options for vision, motor, hearing, and cognitive abilities. To enable VoiceOver on your Mac, press the Esc key on your keyboard. Additionally, by triple-clicking Touch ID, additional accessibility options can be accessed.

Establish a Wi-Fi connection. Select your Wi-Fi network and, if prompted, input its password. Additionally, you may select Other Network Options and adhere to the on-screen guidance when utilizing Ethernet. When connecting the Ethernet cable to the USB-C port on the MacBook Air, an additional Ethernet adapter is required. For instance, the Belkin USB-C to Gigabit Ethernet Adapter may be utilized.

To alter the Wi-Fi network at a later time, select a network as well as input its password, if required, by clicking the Wi-Fi status symbol 📶 within the menu

46

bar or by opening System Settings and selecting Wi-Fi from the sidebar.

After configuration, the Wi-Fi status symbol 🛜 can be added to the menu bar if it is absent. Navigate to System Preferences, select "Control Centre" from the sidebar, and then "Show in Menu Bar" to enable Wi-Fi.

Transfer Data From A Different Mac

Data from another Mac, including but not limited to files, contacts, and accounts, can be migrated to the new MacBook Air. Additionally, you have the option of transferring data from a startup disc or a Time Machine backup that is stored on your Mac. You have the option of wirelessly transferring information from another Mac to the MacBook Air or connecting the Mac to your device via an Ethernet cable.

An information transfer from a Mac is enabled via a checkbox on a Setup Assistant interface titled "Migration Assistant."

Before embarking. Ensure that the software on the second Mac is current and up-to-date. Launch Migration Assistant on the Mac from which the transfer is being initiated. The location of Migration Assistant within the Applications folder is the Utilities folder.

Wireless data transfer. Wirelessly transfer data from a prior Mac to your new Mac if the two devices are nearby. On the configuration interface, select the second Mac and proceed with the provided instructions.

Data transfer is performed via Ethernet cable. Connect your Mac to the other Mac in a direct manner by utilizing an Ethernet cable. To connect the Ethernet cable to the USB-C port on your MacBook Air, you will need an Ethernet adapter, such as the Belkin USB-C to Gigabit Ethernet Adapter. Port-specific, an adapter might be required to connect the Ethernet cable to the other Mac. Select the other Mac with the configuration interface and proceed with the instructions once they are connected.

Later, transfer the data. Additionally, you may opt not to transfer data at this point. Select Not Now in the Migration Assistant window if this is the case. After setup, transmit data by consulting the transmit your data to your new MacBook Air guide.

Establish An Apple ID And Log In To Your Computer

Sign in with your Apple ID. You will receive a verification code on your other Apple devices when you sign in with your Apple ID during registration. Enter the verification code into the new MacBook Air to continue. You have the option to obtain the verification code via text message or phone call if you do not receive it or do not have the device. "Can't use this number" and adhere to the on-screen prompts if the phone number associated with the Apple ID you use is not operational.

To generate a new Apple ID, select "Create new Apple ID." Conversely, to retrieve a forgotten Apple ID or password, select "Forgot Apple ID or password."

Select Set Up Later if you do not wish to sign in or create a new Apple ID at this time. You can sign in using an Apple ID or generate a new Apple ID after setup. To do so, navigate to System Preferences and select "Sign in with your Apple ID" from the sidebar.

After logging in with an Apple ID, please review the following terms and conditions. To approve, proceed after checking the Agree option.

Establish a computer login. Create an account with a username and password, including your name, that can be utilized to authorize additional actions or access your MacBook Air in the future. If you neglect the password for your computer account, you may include an optional indication. To modify the logon image for your account, click it and then select an alternative.

Create a Computer Account

Fill out the following information to create your computer account.

Full name: Ashley Rico
Account name: ashleyrico
This will be the name of your home folder.
Password:
Hint:
☑ Allow my Apple ID to reset this password

Back   Continue

A Setup Assistant interface containing the text "Create a Computer Account."

Note: Your computer account is distinct from your Apple ID; however, if you enable this option during registration, you can utilize your Apple ID to reset the password to activate your Mac if you ever forget it.

CONVERT IT TO YOUR NEW MAC

When you have previously configured another device running macOS 12 or later, iOS 15 or later, or iPadOS 15 or later, an express configuration screen titled "Make This Your New Mac" will appear. This phase is hidden if you do not possess a Mac, iPad, or iPhone equipped with the appropriate software version (Uncertain of the software version installed on you Mac, iPhone, or iPad.)

Make This Your New Mac allows you to bypass many setup procedures by utilizing the settings that are already recorded in your iCloud account. To maintain your current configuration, select Continue. The configuration procedure proceeds directly to Touch ID as well as Apple Pay.

To modify your new MacBook Air's settings, select Customize Settings and continue to the following step.

Personalize The Security As Well As Privacy Settings Of Your Mac, Activate Screen Time, As Well As Enable Siri
With Location Services enabled. Apps such as Maps can be granted access to your Mac's location. To modify your Location Services options at a later time, navigate to System Preferences, select Privacy & Security from the sidebar, and then select Location Services.

In the absence of activating location services, a screen prompting for the selection of a time zone will appear.

Distribute analytics to Apple and its developers. Determine if diagnostics and data should be transmitted to Apple and if Apple should be permitted to share incident as well as usage data with developers. Open System Preferences, select Privacy and Security from the sidebar, then Analytics and Improvements (scroll down if necessary), and then select Options to modify these settings at a later time.

Configure Screen Time. Screen Time enables you to monitor your MacBook Air's daily as well as weekly usage, set app usage limits, manage children's screen time, and much more. Select Continue to enable Screen Time; otherwise, select Set Up Later. If you opt to configure Screen Time at a later time, navigate to System Preferences and select Screen Time from the sidebar.

Protect your information with FileVault. FileVault aids in the protection of your data. You have the option to enable FileVault for data protection and to have your iCloud account activate the disc if you neglect the password during setup.

Deactivate Siri and "Hey Siri." During setup, you can activate Siri and "Hey Siri" to enable spoken commands. Enable Ask Siri to configure Siri. To configure "Hey Siri," when prompted, utter a series of Siri commands. To enable Siri and "Hey Siri" at a later time, select the desired options from the Siri & Spotlight sidebar within System Settings.

Additionally, you have the option to share audio with Apple to enhance Siri. It is possible to modify the decision to share audio at a later time. Select the desired options by navigating to System Preferences, selecting Privacy & Security from the sidebar, and then selecting Analytics & Improvements (scroll down if necessary).

CHAPTER FOUR

BASIC OPERATIONS ON YOUR MACBOOK AIR

TOUCH ID AND APPLE PAY CONFIGURATION

Touch ID allows you to unlock the MacBook Air, authorize purchases alongside Apple Pay, as well as sign in to select third-party applications. You can add a fingerprint to Touch ID. To establish Touch ID, adhere to the on-screen prompts. To modify Touch ID settings at a later time or to add more fingerprints, access System Settings and select Touch ID & Password from the sidebar. To submit a fingerprint, follow the on-screen instructions after clicking the submit icon $+$.

Establish Apple Pay. You can add a debit, credit, or store card that can be utilized to make transactions alongside Touch ID by configuring Apple Pay as well as entering the card information and following the on-screen instructions. You may be required to verify the card you currently employ for media purchases.

To configure Apple Pay or subsequently add more cards, navigate to System Preferences and select

Wallet and Apple Pay. Utilize the on-screen instructions to configure Apple Pay.

Please be advised that the eligibility of your card for use with Apple Pay is determined by the card issuer, who may request supplementary information from you to finalize the verification procedure. A multitude of debit and credit cards are compatible with Apple Pay.

Configure The Desktop's Appearance
Select your style. Choose between Light, Dark, or Auto to customize the appearance of your desktop. If you wish to modify a setting you made during installation at a later time, navigate to System Preferences, pick Appearance, and afterward select an option. Additionally, other appearance parameters can be modified, including the size of auxiliary icons and the color of the highlights.

Note: This stage is omitted if you opt for express configuration with Make This Your New Mac.

Setup Is Finished
The upgraded MacBook Air is now operational.

ONCE THE CONFIGURATION OF YOUR
MACBOOK AIR IS COMPLETE

You can now begin customizing your MacBook Air once the setup process is complete. Commence the process of customizing your Mac by initiating the creation of email as well as calendar accounts, modifying the text display by enlarging text and other elements on the screen, or altering the desktop image. Acquire the knowledge necessary to utilize your MacBook Air in concert with other gadgets made by Apple by studying Work with various gadgets as well as Share content between gadgets. Learn more regarding the Apps on the MacBook Air or how to install fresh applications, which include previously purchased iPad and iPhone apps, on your Mac through the App Store if you have an interest in applications. (Note that while the iPhone as well as iPad app store is extensive, it does not carry every app.)

Check out the Tips section for your Mac. Launch Finder, and select "Tips for your Mac" from the Help menu that appears under Help.

Ultimately, familiarize yourself with your brand-new MacBook Air. Examine the terminals, integrated camera, and additional hardware characteristics in Take a Tour: MacBook Air with M3 chip or Take a Tour: MacBook Air with M2 chip. Explore the functionalities of the Magic Keyboard while gaining knowledge of and modifying gestures using the Trackpad. Additionally, you have the option to link an external display or wireless accessories, such as an additional keyboard or mouse, to your MacBook Air via the Use accessories option.

APPLE ID ON A MAC

An Apple ID grants you access to every Apple service as an account. Utilize your Apple ID for the following: download applications from the App Store; access media within Apple Podcasts, Apple Music, Apple TV, as well as Apple Books; configure a Family Sharing group; and maintain content across gadgets via iCloud.

Additionally, you can access other applications and websites with your Apple ID.

Important: You do not need to establish a new Apple ID if you forget your Apple ID password; simply select "Forgot Apple ID or password? In the sign-in window, click the "link to retrieve password."

Each family member should have an Apple ID if other family members use Apple devices. Family Sharing, which is described later in this section, allows you to establish Apple ID accounts for your children and share purchases and subscriptions.

Everything is in one location. Oversee all aspects of the Apple ID you use from a single location. Launch the System Preferences menu on your MacBook Air. Located at the highest point of the sidebar are the Apple ID as well as Family Sharing settings. If you are not already logged in with your Apple ID, select "Sign in with your Apple ID" from the menu at the top of the page.

Manage family members, parental controls, purchases, and more.

Update account information.

Turn on iCloud features

Manage media accounts.

See all devices signed in with your Apple ID.

The Apple ID configurations located in System Settings include prominently displayed options for managing media accounts, updating account information, enabling or disabling iCloud features, and controlling purchases and family members.

Payment, security, and account information should be updated. Select an item from the sidebar of System Settings labeled "Apple ID" to access and modify the account information associated with that ID.

❖ **Context:** Indicates whether your account is configured and operating appropriately; if it is not, it provides suggestions and alerts.

❖ **Personal Information**: Modify the details associated with the Apple ID that you use including your name, date of birth, emoji, or photo. Additionally, establish communication preferences with Apple and gain insight into the management of your data.

❖ **Sign-In and Security**: Modify the password associated with your Apple ID, enable two-factor authentication, modify the email addresses and phone numbers that can be utilized for login purposes, and establish Account Recovery or Legacy Contact.

❖ **Payment as well as shipment**: Oversee the payment methods as well as the shipment address associated with the Apple ID you use to make transactions from the Apple Store.

❖ In the iCloud menu, select the desired iCloud features after clicking iCloud. In addition, iCloud+ features can be activated as well and iCloud storage can be managed. Your content is stored in iCloud when you enable an iCloud feature; therefore, you can access any material on any gadget with an iCloud connection and the same Apple ID.

❖ **Media and Purchases:** Oversee the subscriptions, administer the accounts associated with Apple Music, Apple Podcasts, Apple TV, as well as Apple Books, and configure the purchasing settings.

The Apple ID Password & Security option within System Preferences. You can configure Account Recovery and Legacy Contact from this page.

Access every one of your devices. You can view the status of iCloud Backup for an iOS or iPadOS gadget, as well as the devices associated with your Apple ID. Additionally, you can confirm that Find My [device] is enabled for every gadget (see Find My), or remove a gadget from your account if you no longer own it.

Conspiracy within the family. Family Sharing enables the formation of groups of up to six individuals. Subsequently, devices can be marked as misplaced or shared in Find My. Additionally, you can regulate your children's device usage by enrolling them in Apple ID programs and imposing Screen Time restrictions.

Family Sharing allows for the sharing of subscriptions, such as iCloud+, Apple TV+, and Apple Music. Additionally, purchases made through the App Store, Apple TV app, Apple Books, and iTunes Store can be shared. Family members are permitted to maintain individual iCloud accounts. One credit card can be used to pay for family purchases, and expenditures by children can be authorized directly from the MacBook Air. To manage the settings for Family Sharing, navigate to Family within System Preferences.

IMPLEMENT ICLOUD ON YOUR MACBOOK AIR

iCloud enables users to maintain current information across all their devices and facilitates collaboration with family and colleagues. When you enroll in each of your Apple Watch, iPhone, iPad, or iPod touch using the same Apple ID and iCloud, your MacBook Air will operate in perfect harmony with these devices.

If iCloud was not enabled during the initial setup of your Mac, navigate to System Preferences and select "Sign in with your Apple ID" from the sidebar. Once logged in, select iCloud and then toggle iCloud features to the desired state.

Content accessibility across devices. You can ensure that you are always current by storing, editing, and sharing your documents, photographs, as well as videos across gadgets in a secure manner using iCloud. Consult Access your iCloud content on your Mac to begin.

Macbook Air compatibility with additional devices. Utilize Continuity to transfer material between the MacBook Air and various other gadgets seamlessly. Simply sign in with your Apple ID on each device, and your MacBook Air and other nearby devices will collaborate in convenient ways. For example, one can initiate a task on one device and complete it on another, employ an iPhone as a webcam for a MacBook Air, utilize AirPlay to mirror the screen of an iPad to another Mac or Apple TV, configure Sidecar to enable iPad-to-Mac collaboration and accomplish additional tasks.

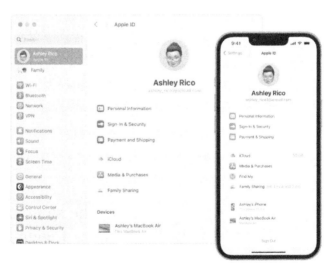

iCloud configurations on a Mac and an iPhone.

Benefit from iCloud+ more. A subscription to iCloud+ grants you additional storage space for photographs, files, and other types of content. iCloud+ storage plans can be shared via Family Sharing. iCloud+ additionally provides access to HomeKit Secure Video, iCloud Private Relay, and custom email domains for mail addresses on iCloud.com.

MAC ACCESS TO YOUR ICLOUD CONTENT

iCloud facilitates the safeguarding, updating, and accessibility of critical data, including but not limited to photographs, files, notes, and iCloud Keychain, across all of your devices. It is pre-installed on all Apple devices and provides each user with 5 GB of storage space. (Attainments from the iTunes Store, program Store, Apple TV program, or Apple Books do not contribute to the total amount of available space.)

Therefore, if you own an iPhone, iPad, or iPod touch, simply sign in with your Apple ID and enable iCloud on each device, and you will have access to everything you require. If you require additional storage space as well as additional benefits such as iCloud Private Relay, Hide My Email, Custom Email Domain, as well as HomeKit Secure Video support, you may upgrade to iCloud+.

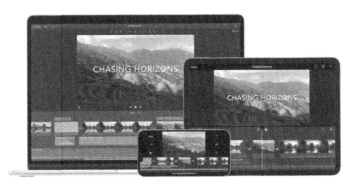

Display of identical content on an iPhone, a MacBook Air, as well as an iPad.

iCloud Drive will automatically back up your desktop as well as the Documents subdirectory. Files that are saved in the Documents folder or on the desktop become instantly accessible on iCloud Drive as well as can be accessed from any location. You can access files stored on various devices when using iCloud Drive: your MacBook Air, your iPhone or iPad via the Files application, the iCloud.com website, or a Windows PC using the iCloud for Windows application. Anywhere you access the file from your gadget or iCloud Drive, any modifications you make to the file will be reflected.

Launch iCloud Drive by navigating to System Preferences, selecting your Apple ID within the sidebar, then clicking iCloud.

Share and store photographs. iCloud storage enables you to access your photo library and videos, along with any modifications you apply to them, across all of your devices. To enable iCloud Photos, navigate to System Preferences, select your Apple ID from the sidebar, select iCloud, and then toggle Photos on.

Up to five additional users can access and share pictures and videos via iCloud Shared Photo Library. Any user can modify the shared library by adding new content, editing existing content, or adding comments. It is simple to incorporate specific photographs from your collection, including those taken on a particular date or featuring a particular person, via intelligent suggestions. Navigate to Photos > Settings, select the Shared Library tab, and finally adhere to the on-screen prompts to begin.

Purchases can be enjoyed anywhere. Purchases made through the App Store, Apple TV app, Apple Books, as well as iTunes Store, are accessible at any time when you are signed in to all of your gadgets with the identical Apple ID. This regardless of the device or machine used to make the purchase also applies to these purchases. This allows you to access your music, movies, publications, and more from anywhere.

Determine the location of your MacBook Air by using Find My Mac. If Find My Mac is enabled and the MacBook Air you're using is missing, you can use it to lock its display, delete its data remotely, or locate it on a map. To enable Find My Mac, navigate to System Preferences, select iCloud, then Find My Mac, and then enter your Apple ID in the sidebar.

Note: Find My Mac can only be enabled on a single user account if your MacBook Air supports multiple accounts.

MENU BAR AND DESKTOP OF YOUR MAC

The desktop appears as soon as the MacBook Air boots up. The port is situated at the bottom of the display, while the navigational bar runs along the highest point.

The Apple menu, the App menu, the Help menu, the desktop, a Finder window, the menu bar, the Wi-Fi symbol, the System Settings symbol, the Finder symbol, as well as the Dock are displayed on a Mac screen.

Unable to locate the cursor on the display? Temporarily enlarge it by swiftly tracing your finger back and forth across the display. Alternatively, utilize a mouse and rapidly slide it back and forth.

Desktop computer. You perform your tasks on the desktop, including accessing and utilizing applications, editing files, and conducting web or MacBook Air searches with Spotlight, among others. Select a desktop image by navigating to System Preferences, selecting Wallpaper from the sidebar, and then selecting an option. Additionally, files can be stored on the desktop and organized through the use of layers.

The menu bar is present. Placing along the highest point of the display is the menu bar. Utilize the menus located on the left to select commands and execute duties within applications. The menu products vary based on the application being utilized. Utilize the symbols on the right to establish a connection to a Wi-Fi network 📶, access Control Centre, verify battery charge (by selecting the symbol labeled "Full Battery 🔋'"), conduct searches using Spotlight (by selecting "Spotlight 🔍"), and for additional functionalities.

It is possible to modify the elements that manifest in the menu pane.

The Apple catalogue . The Apple menu, which is consistently located in the upper-left corner of the display, comprises frequently utilized products. To launch it, simply tap the Apple icon .

The application interface. It is possible to manage multiple applications and windows concurrently. Following the Apple menu, the name of the active application is displayed in italics to the right, followed by the app's menus. When a new application is launched or a window within an existing app is clicked, both the name of the app menu, as well as the menus contained within it, are updated to reflect the new application. If you are unable to locate a command in a menu, check the app menu to determine if the desired app is active.

Assistance menu. Constant assistance for the MacBook Air can be accessed via the menu bar. To access the macOS User Guide, launch the Finder within the Dock, select Help from the menu, and then click macOS Help. Alternatively, enter your query into the search field as well as select a suggestion. To obtain assistance for a particular application, launch it and select Help from the menu bar.

It is possible to transfer widgets from an iPhone to your desktop via the widget gallery, without the need to download the corresponding application. Go to Manage Windows on a Mac for more information.

A portion of the desktop displays the Help menu, which include the search as well as macOS help options.

FINDER IMPLEMENTED ON A MAC

The Finder, symbolized by a blue icon featuring a jovial visage, serves as the central repository for your Mac. It facilitates the organization and accessibility of virtually all files and folders on your Mac, which includes documents, images, and videos. Select the Finder icon located in the Dock at the bottom of the display to launch Finder. To edit a file, force-click its name. To rapidly inspect its contents, force-click its icon.

An active Finder window in which files and folders are represented by icons.

Obtain organization. Pre-established folders for common categories of content—documents, images, applications, music, and more—are present on your Mac. To maintain organization as you create documents, install applications, and perform other tasks, you can create new folders. Select File > New Folder to establish a fresh folder.

Unite gadgets. A device, such as an iPhone or iPad, is displayed within the Finder sidebar when it is connected. To access the gadget's backup, update, sync, as well as restore options, click the device's name.

The sidebar of Finder. The left-hand sidebar includes the items that you frequently access or wish to activate rapidly. To view all of your iCloud Drive-stored documents, select the corresponding folder from the sidebar. Select the Shared folder to view only the documents which you are the one sharing and which are shared with you. To modify the sidebar's contents, navigate to Finder > Settings.

Modify how files and folders are viewed. To modify how documents and folders are displayed, select the pop-up menu icon located at the highest point of the Finder window. Consider displaying them as icons⊟⊟, in a gallery⊡, a list⊟, or hierarchical columns⊞. By displaying a large preview of the selected file in both Gallery View as well as Column View, it is possible to visually distinguish images, videos, and other documents. Additionally, you can readily perform modifications such as rotating or annotating an image. To display the options for the Preview pane in the Finder, select View > Show Preview. To modify the appearance of the preview, select View > Show Preview Options and then the appropriate options for the file type.

To display filenames in Gallery View, select "Show filename" by pressing Command-J.

An open Finder window within Gallery View displays a sizable image accompanied by a series of smaller images—the scrubber bar—below it. Rotation, marking, and additional controls are located on the scrubber bar's right.

Prompt Reactions. Select More in Column View or Gallery View to access shortcuts for editing and managing files directly within the Finder. These shortcuts appear in the bottom right corner of the Finder window. One can perform various operations on an image, including cropping and annotating, combining images as well as PDFs into a single file, rotating images, executing shortcuts generated by the Shortcuts application, and establishing custom actions via Automator workflows (e.g., watermarking a file.

A Brief Look. Click the Space bar while selecting a file to launch Quick Look. Without launching a distinct application, sign PDFs, trim videos and audio recordings, and annotate, rotate, and crop images using the icons located at the highest point of the Quick Look window.

Alternative image descriptions that are comprehensible by VoiceOver can be included via Markup in Preview or Quick Look.

Get there more quickly. Using the Go option in the Finder menu bar, it is possible to access locations and folders quickly. Select Go > Utilities to access the Utilities folder without the need for multiple clicks. You may also navigate to the upper level of nested folders by selecting Go > Enclosing Folder. To navigate to a particular folder, select Go > Go to Folder and enter the path you know.

THE MACINTOSH DOCK

The Dock, located at the bottom of the display, serves as a practical location to organize frequently used applications and documents.

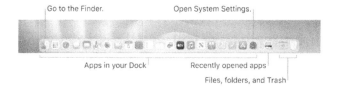

The Dock contains the Finder, System Preferences, and a divider for distinguishing applications from files and folders.

Launch a program or file. To view all the applications installed on your Mac, select the

Launchpad icon ⣿ in the Dock, followed by the desired application. Additionally, it is possible to conduct a Spotlight search Q for an application (located in the upper-right corner of the menu bar) and launch the application directly from the results. Apps that were recently launched are displayed in the Dock's center section.

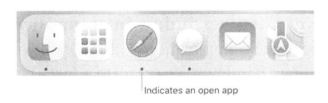

Indicates an open app

A segment of the Dock contains black marks below active applications.

Close a program. When the red dot in the upper-left corner of an active window is clicked, the window is closed while the application remains open. A black dot appears beneath open applications in the Dock. Control-click the app symbol within the Dock and select Quit to terminate it.

An item is added to the Dock. Drop the item in the desired location by dragging it. Place applications in the Dock's left section, followed by files and folders in the right.

Eliminate an object from the Dock. Remove it by dragging it from the Dock. The item remains in the Dock of the MacBook Air and is not physically removed.

Observe all active applications on your Mac.
To access Mission Control, press the Mission Control key⊟☐ on your keyboard or gesture with three fingers on your trackpad. Navigate between your active windows, desktop areas, full-screen applications, and more. Additionally, the Mission Control symbol⊞ can be added to the Dock.

View every active window in an application. A force-click on an application in the Dock will reveal all of its open windows. To perform a force click, click and press more deeply.

Mouse over Desktop & Dock in the System Preferences to modify the Dock's appearance and behavior. Customize the Dock's dimensions, position it to the left or right of the screen, and configure it to conceal when not in use, among other options.

CENTRE FOR NOTIFICATIONS ON YOUR MAC

Notification Centre consolidates in a single location all of your vital data, reminders, and widgets. Access information regarding calendar events, commodities, the weather, and more; also, review any missing notifications (emails, messages, reminders, as well as more).

Launch the Notification Centre application. Tap the date or time displayed in the upper-right corner of the display, or use two fingertips to move left from the right margin of the trackpad. Continue scrolling to view more.

Notification Centre with widgets and notifications for ScreenTime, Photos, Home, and Calendar.

Attempt to concentrate on what you are doing. Focus can automatically filter notifications so that you only see those you specify when you're working, having dinner, or simply don't want to be disturbed. Focus can halt all notifications or only select ones, and it can notify contacts via Message status that your notifications have been silenced. To configure Focus, navigate to System Preferences and select Focus from the sidebar. To enable or disable Focus, select a Focus from the Control Centre symbol in the menu bar, followed by the Focus section.

You can personalize a Focus to reflect your current activity and enable notifications for forthcoming events, phone calls, and apps from specific users or applications, among other things. In addition to sharing your Focus across devices, you can conceal distracting content in applications such as Calendar and Messages using Focus filters.

Engage in conversation regarding your notifications. Respond to an email, examine information about upcoming calendar events, or listen to the most recent podcast. To view options, perform an action, or obtain additional information, click the arrow located in the upper-right quadrant of the notification.

Configure the notification settings. To customize which notifications are displayed, navigate to System Preferences and select Notifications. The order of notifications is by date of receipt.

Personalize the elements. To access the widget gallery, locate Edit Widgets (located at the bottom of all your notifications) and utilize it to rearrange, add, or eliminate widgets. You may use the same Apple ID on both your Mac and iPhone to add widgets to your desktop, eliminating the need to install the necessary applications on your Mac. In the Notification Centre or anywhere else on your desktop, you can drag new widgets. You may also utilize App Store widgets from third parties.

CONTROL CENTRE ON YOUR MAC

Control Centre consolidates all additional menu bar options into a single location, providing quick access from the menu bar to the most frequently used controls, such as those for Bluetooth, AirDrop, Mic Mode, Screen Mirroring, Focus, brightness, and volume. To access the Control Centre, click the icon located within the upper-right corner of the display.

To view additional options, click. Select an option by clicking an icon. To access Wi-Fi Settings, view your preferred networks, or access other networks, for instance, select the Wi-Fi icon. Click the Control Centre icon once more to return to the primary Control Centre interface.

The Control Centre on your Mac is highlighted with a callout to the Display icon while zoomed in.

Organize the interface. Utilize Stage Manager to organize your applications and windows automatically and toggle between them with ease. You can also construct workflow-optimal workstations by grouping applications.

Observe the mic. The recording indicator indicates whether or not the microphone on your computer is active or has been recently utilized. This light enhances the security and privacy of your Mac by notifying you when an application attempts to access the microphone.

Pinch your preferred Control Centre items. By dragging a preferred item from the Control Centre to the menu bar, you can pin it for quick access alongside a single click. To modify the contents of the menu bar, access the Control Centre settings and select "Show in Menu Bar" from the navigation menu next to each module. A preview of the location of the control within the menu bar is displayed. Certain elements in the menu bar and Control Centre are immutable.

To remove an item from the options bar rapidly, hold down the Command key while dragging the item out from the menu bar.

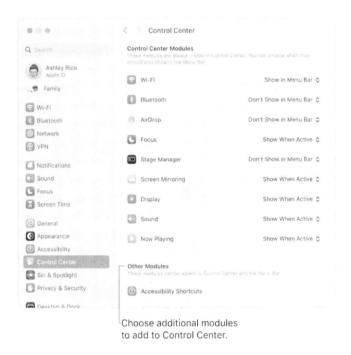

Choose additional modules
to add to Control Center.

The Control Centre window for configuring parameters.

SPOTLIGHT ON THE MACINTOSH

Utilize the Spotlight icon $\mathcal{Q}$ to quickly locate any item, including documents, contacts, calendar events, images, as well as email messages, on the MacBook Air. Spotlight can also be used to launch applications or execute fast operations, such as setting a timer.

Search any term. Commence typing by clicking the Spotlight emblem $\mathcal{Q}$ in the upper-right corner of the display. Additionally, the Spotlight key (F4) on the keyboard can be utilized. Live Text enables Spotlight to conduct text searches within images. Languages other than those specified are unavailable.

Use the Command–Space bar to toggle the Spotlight search field's visibility to hidden.

The Spotlight window displays "horse photos" search results.

Launch an application. With the application's name entered in Spotlight, select Return.

Execute rapid actions. Spotlight enables the execution of specific operations, such as initiating a Focus, executing a shortcut, or establishing an alarm. Launch Spotlight and search for the desired action. Enter Clock followed by Create Timer, for example, to establish a timer directly from Spotlight.

A Spotlight search for "timer" returns results that can be accessed via the Create Timer fast action.

Perform currency, temperature, and unit conversions. Enter a quantity and a currency (such as $, €, or ⁻), then select Return to obtain a list of converted values. For conversions between units of measurement, specify an alternative.

Reduce the scope of your inquiry. Spotlight queries can selectively include or exclude particular folders, discs, or categories of information (e.g., messages or emails). In the "Search results" section of the "Siri & Spotlight" menu in the System Settings, deselect or re-select the categories that you wish to have included or omitted from the Spotlight results.

Implement Siri Suggestions. Spotlight searches generate Siri Suggestions that include information from Wikipedia articles, web search results, news, sports, weather, equities, and entertainment, among other sources.

To restrict Spotlight to items found exclusively on the MacBook Air, navigate to System Preferences, select Siri & Spotlight, and then deselect Siri Suggestions from the Search Results. Additionally, you can modify the categories that Spotlight searches for.

USING SIRI ON A MAC

On your MacBook Air, you can turn on Siri with your voice and utilize it for a variety of duties. You can, for instance, add items to the calendar, schedule meetings, modify settings, receive responses, send messages, and make phone conversations. Siri can provide information, directions ("How do I get home from here?"), and fundamental tasks (e.g., "Create a new grocery list"). It can also generate a new grocery list as well as carry out a variety of other useful functions.

By activating the "Listen for" feature in the Siri settings, Siri will respond to your calls and messages "Hey Siri" or "Siri" without delay.

Your Mac needs to be linked to the internet to utilize Siri. Siri's availability may be limited to specific regions or languages, with potential variations in its features across cultures.

Activate and switch on Siri. Configure options via System Preferences, Siri & Spotlight within the sidebar. To activate Siri, hold down the Dictation/Siri (F5) key on the microphone key, if Siri was enabled during setup. Alternatively, in System Settings, pick Siri & Spotlight, then select Ask Siri. Other Siri settings include the accent and language to be used, as well as whether or not Siri should be displayed in the menu pane.

The Siri preferences window with Ask Siri enabled, along with several customization options on the right.

To add the Siri symbol to the menu bar, navigate to the Control Centre settings and select that option. To utilize Siri, simply select the Siri icon.

Siri, or "Hey Siri." You can obtain responses to your inquiries by simply saying "Hey Siri" or "Siri" on your MacBook Air. In the "Listen for" menu of System Settings, select the phrase you wish to use Siri to recognize, then click Siri & Spotlight. When prompted, perform a series of Siri commands verbally.

To enhance usability, the "Hey Siri" function remains inactive when the MacBook Air's lid is closed. While linked to an external display with the lid closed, Siri can still be activated via the menu bar icon.

Enter text into Siri. Enter your commands into Siri as opposed to voicing them. In the System Preferences, navigate to Accessibility, then tap Siri on the right to enable "Type to Siri."

Display Captions. Display the words spoken by Siri on the screen. Navigate to System Preferences, select Siri & Spotlight, then select Siri Responses, and enable "Always display Siri captions." Additionally, "Always show speech" can be enabled to have Siri transcribe your commands.

Utilize drag-and-drop. Utilize the Siri window to drag and drop locations and images into a text message, email, or document. Text can also be copied and pasted.

Alter your tone of voice. In the System Settings menu, select Siri & Spotlight, then select an option within the Siri Voice menu.

Throughout this guide, you will encounter recommendations for Siri-related tasks; they appear as follows:

Query Siri. Say the following:

❖ "Preside over my reminders."
❖ "What time does it currently stand in Paris?"

SYSTEM PREFERENCES FOR THE MAC

System Preferences provides the ability to personalize and alter the settings of your MacBook

Air to suit your specific requirements. For instance, you can modify the luminance or resolution of the display, add a screen saver that also functions as your wallpaper, control and share passwords, and alter accessibility settings, among other things. Additionally, the latest software update can be downloaded.

Click the System Preferences icon in the Dock or select Apple > System Preferences, then select the desired setting from the sidebar to begin. Swipe downward to view every setting in the sidebar.

If you are uncertain where to locate a specific setting that you wish to modify, utilize the search field. As you input, results emerge in the sidebar.

The System Settings window is labeled Appearance.

Secure the screen. After an amount of inactivity, you can configure your MacBook Air to switch off the display or initiate a screen saver. A password can also be implemented to reestablish access to the screen upon your return to the Mac. Navigate to Lock Screen within System Preferences to configure.

Select a desktop saver. As well as serving as a wallpaper, slow-motion screen savers can elevate the appearance of the MacBook Air's display to a work of art when you're not using it. Navigate to Screen Saver in System Preferences to configure. You can transform a Landscape, Cityscape, Underwater, Earth, or Shuffle Aerials screen saver into a wallpaper by selecting "Show as wallpaper."

Bear in mind your credentials. You have the option to access credentials stored in iCloud Keychain or on your Mac through System Preferences. After selecting Passwords from the sidebar, input your MacBook Air login credentials. To view your site-specific password, hover your mouse pointer over the information icon ⓘ followed by the password. Additionally, you may modify or remove your password, or you may select the information symbol to convey it via AirDrop.

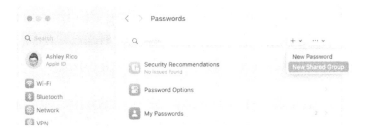

The System Settings credentials pane displays a collection of credentials that are shared among three individuals.

Passwords and credentials should be shared with others. Create a group of trusted individuals with access to the shared credentials and passkeys. When modifications are implemented, passwords and passkeys remain current. Navigate to System Preferences, then select Passwords. Select New Shared Group ⊤ from the Add menu, then enter the group's name before clicking Add People. Select Add once the names of the individuals with whom you wish to share have been entered. To distribute passwords to the group, select the group ⊤, press Move Passwords to a Group from the Add menu, then select the accounts whose passwords you wish to distribute as well as click Move.

Make adjustments to the Control Centre and menu pane. Select which configurations you desire to be displayed in the menu bar or Control Centre. Select the desired options by selecting Control Centre from the sidebar of System Settings.

Update macOS. Click General in System Preferences, then Software Update to determine whether or not your Mac is operating the most recent version of macOS software. Options regarding automatic software updates can be specified.

Configuration of iCloud and family sharing. Configure and oversee Family Sharing, sign in to iCloud with the Apple ID you use on the MacBook Air and manage how your applications utilize iCloud. Consult Apple ID on Mac and Utilize iCloud with the MacBook Air for additional details.

CONFIGURATION OPTIONS FOR YOUR MAC

Contrast the illumination of your environment. Your MacBook Air is equipped with True Tone. For an enhanced natural viewing experience, True Tone automatically adjusts the display's color to correspond with the ambient light. Activate or deactivate True Tone via the Displays menu in System Preferences.

Bypass static desktops. Utilizing a dynamic desktop image synchronizes the desktop image with the current time of day in the user's location. In the System Preferences menu, select Wallpaper, then select an image for Dynamic Desktop. To adjust the time on your display according to your time zone, activate Location Services. Disabling Location Services causes the displayed image to adjust following the time zone configured within the Date and Time settings.

Simplify the visibility of your display. To optimize visibility, one may adjust the screen's resolution to enlarge all elements on the screen or enlarge text and icons to enhance their scale. Additionally, you can enhance the visibility of the pointer or rapidly locate it by performing a mouse motion.

Keep your attention with Dark Mode. It is possible to apply a dark color scheme to the Dock, desktop, menu bar, and all native macOS applications. Your content is prominently displayed, whereas dimmed controls and windows diminish into the background. Applications such as Mail, Contacts, Calendar, as well as Messages feature white text on a black background to improve legibility in low-light environments.

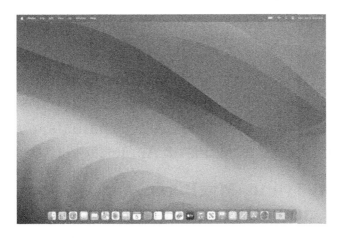

The dark mode interface.

For professionals who alter images and photos, Dark Mode has been meticulously optimized to highlight colors and intricate details against the app's dark backgrounds. However, it's also ideal for those who wish to concentrate solely on their content.

During the night shift. In low-light conditions or at night, change the color temperature of your Mac to milder tones to reduce your exposure to bright blue light. Because blue light can hinder the ability to fall asleep, milder screen tones may contribute to a more restful night's sleep. Night Shift can be programmed to autonomously switch on and off at predetermined intervals, or to remain on from sunset to sunrise. Navigate to Displays in System Settings, then select the Night Shift icon at the bottom to configure the desired settings. Utilize the slider to modify the temperature of the color.

Integrate a display. A TV, projector, or external display can be connected to a Mac.

TIME SPENT ON A MAC

Screen Time provides tools that facilitate pausing during idleness, displays the amount of time spent on a MacBook Air, as well as enables parents to monitor their children's activities on Apple gadgets.

Observe your MacBook Air in use. Access reports that detail the amount of time spent on applications and websites on a daily or weekly basis, the apps that send you the most notifications, and the frequency at which you take up the gadget each day. Select Screen Time from the sidebar of System

Preferences, followed by App and Website Activity, Notifications, or Pickups. Screen Time might require to be enabled before the appearance of these options.

A Screen Time settings interface that provides options to manage Screen Time, including designating downtime, establishing application as well as communication limits, as well as viewing App Usage, Notifications, as well as Pickups.

Establish limits. Implement time restrictions on particular applications, app categories, and websites. Select Downtime from Screen Time, enable Downtime, and then select the Schedule pop-up option to generate a daily or weekly schedule that is unique to that day.

Watch over your child's screen time. Screen Time can be configured by parents on the Mac, iPhone, or iPad so that everything is optimized for their children's devices. Media ratings based on age can also be configured for the Books as well as Music applications.

Avoid overlooking crucial details. Determine which websites and applications you must have constant access to. Select Always Allowed from the Screen Time menu, then activate the applications you wish to have accessible during inactivity.

CHAPTER FIVE

MORE FUNCTIONALITY ON A MAC

The accessibility tools included on your Mac make Apple functions accessible and simple to use for everyone. To gain access to these tools, select Accessibility from the sidebar of System Preferences. Accessibility configurations fall into the following five categories:

❖ **Vision:** Increase the size of the pointer, magnify the display, and apply color filters, among other things.

❖ **Hearing:** Display and modify on-screen captions, initiate and get back Real-Time Text (RTT) conversations, obtain real-time audio captions, and more.

❖ **Mobility:** Utilize assistive devices, spoken commands, keys on the keyboard, an on-screen keypad, or facial expressions to operate your Mac and applications.

❖ **Speech:** Transmit your text to a speaker and then have it spoken aloud. Additionally, you can generate your accent.

❖ In general, one can modify keyboard shortcuts to expeditiously activate or deactivate accessibility functions.

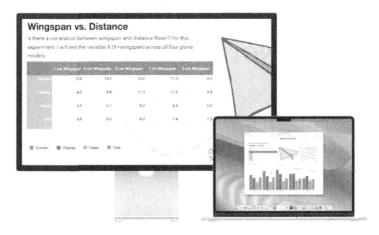

Zoom Active display on the desktop, with a fixed size of the screen on the MacBook Air.

Make View Adjustments with Zoom. You may magnify a portion or the entire display. If you own multiple monitors, you can maintain one at its default resolution and the other at a high magnification. To modify the magnification settings, select Apple > System Preferences, then magnification from the sidebar after selecting Accessibility.

Utilize VoiceOver, the integrated screen reader. VoiceOver provides verbal descriptions of on-screen content and reads audibly the text in Windows, documents, as well as webpages. VoiceOver enables gesture control of your Mac via the trackpad or keyboard. Additionally, a refreshable braille display can be connected for use with VoiceOver.

VoiceOver can also be used to:

- ❖ Include alternative picture descriptions that are VoiceOver-readable.
- ❖ Incorporate personalized descriptions into PDF signatures.
- ❖ Utilize iCloud for storing custom punctuation marks.
- ❖ Select from an assortment of international braille tables.

Employ Siri to operate VoiceOver. If you desire Siri to speak in your natural tone, you have the option between VoiceOver and Speech.

To activate VoiceOver, perform one of the subsequent:

- ❖ Enter the command F5. SoundOver can be deactivated by tapping the keys if it has already been on.
- ❖ Apply Siri. Say something along the lines of "Activate VoiceOver" or "Deactivate VoiceOver."
- ❖ Touch ID can be activated by holding down the Command key on a Mac or Magic Keyboard whilst rapidly pressing Touch ID three times.
- ❖ Select Accessibility from the sidebar that appears after selecting Apple > System Settings (you may need to navigate down). To toggle VoiceOver on or off, select VoiceOver from the menu on the right.

Slightly magnify words by utilizing Hover Text. When you select Command while the pointer is poised over text, a window containing magnified text will appear on the display.

The Hover Text function enlarges the selected text within a new window.

Adjust the colors of the Mac display. The colors of your Mac's interface can be modified via color filter options. Navigate to Apple > System Preferences, select Accessibility from the sidebar, and then select Display to modify these options. (Depth may require the user to navigate.) Change the value of this option to enable or disable the ability to distinguish colors rapidly via the Accessibility Options. Option-Command-F5 will bring you to these settings; if the Mac or Magic Keyboard supports Touch ID, tap Touch ID three times rapidly.

HEARING ACCESSIBILITY CHARACTERISTICS

Caption content in real-time. Live captioning (beta) enables the addition of captioning in real-time to audio, video, as well as conversations.

Essential: Live Captions is not accessible in all countries, regions, or languages at this time due to its beta status. Live caption accuracy is subject to variation as well as should not be trusted during critical or life-threatening circumstances.

Overcome undesired din. Reduce distractions as well as obfuscate undesirable environmental pollution with soothing sounds such as the ocean or rain. Opt for background audio by navigating to Apple > System Preferences, selecting Accessibility from the sidebar, followed by selecting Audio. Adjust the amplitude of the background sound by selecting from an assortment of sounds and manipulating the slider.

MOBILITY ACCESSIBILITY CHARACTERISTICS

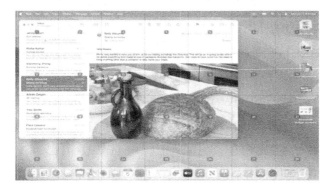

Utilize your voice to operate your Mac. Voice Control enables the execution of an extensive variety of commands through vocal means. Because the processing of all audio for Voice Control occurs on your Mac, your private information is protected. Select Apple Menu > System Preferences, then select Accessibility within the sidebar, followed by Voice Control on the right, to enable Voice Control.

❖ **Vocalize your typing**: Invoke "Dictation mode" to dictate individual words. Any verbal expressions not intended for voice control purposes are recorded as text. Additionally "Spelling mode" can be used to dictate each character.

❖ Rich text editing enables you to make corrections rapidly: You can substitute phrases, position the cursor to make changes, and select text precisely. Consider modifying the phrase "John will soon be there" to "John has just arrived." When choosing the correct words, suggested words and emoji assist you in selecting the desired item swiftly.

❖ **Launch and interact with applications**: Launch and interact with applications using voice commands. Items are selectable via click, navigate down, or select. Display the Commands window by saying "Show commands" if you are uncertain which commands are available. You may also say "show numbers" followed by the number you wish to select to display a number notation next to each interactive item. If you need to manipulate a portion of the display without a control, you may select "show grid" to have a grid appear over it, allowing you to perform operations such as clicking, zooming, dragging, and more.

Custom orthography can be dictated letter by letter, and additional custom terms can be added to assist Voice Control in recognizing frequently used words. Add the desired words by navigating to System Preferences > Accessibility, selecting Voice Control, and then clicking Vocabulary. To modify commands, choose Commands from the Voice Control settings page, then choose whether to retain default commands or add new ones.

Personalize the indicator. The outline as well as fill color of the mouse pointer are customizable to facilitate identification of its movement as well as shape changes.

Enhancements to keyboard accessibility. An expanded set of keyboard shortcuts enables one to operate all aspects of the Mac using only the keyboard, eliminating the need for a mouse or trackpad.

Speech Accessibility Characteristics
Permit your Mac to communicate. You can dictate your thoughts aloud via Live Speech during FaceTime and phone interactions, in addition to in-person discussions. Preserve frequently used

expressions for fast reference during discussions. A voice can be selected for use, or a personal voice can be recorded. Refer to Create a Personal Voice in the User Guide for macOS.

ESTABLISH CONNECTIONS WITH OTHERS

Utilizing FaceTime alongside additional videoconferencing applications on the MacBook Air enables you to communicate with others.

Employ FaceTime

Whether you are at home or abroad, you can use FaceTime to communicate with an individual or an entire group, irrespective of the devices they are using. Additionally, you can make and receive calls directly from the MacBook Air via Wi-Fi. Additionally, both sending and receiving text messages are possible.

A FaceTime group conversation.

Apply FaceTime to a communication. FaceTime HD video conversations can be initiated using the Mac's integrated camera. FaceTime after entering the name, phone number, or email address of the recipient into the New FaceTime field. To make an audio-only call when video calls are inconvenient, select FaceTime Audio from the pop-up menu. Upon receiving a FaceTime invitation, the option to participate via audio or video is presented.

FaceTime can be used in groups. In a group call, you can communicate with up to 32 individuals. Generate an exclusive hyperlink for dissemination among a group. Select Link Creation. Transfer the hyperlink to your Clipboard or distribute it to your acquaintances via Messages or Mail. FaceTime conversations can now be joined via a link on devices other than Apple products.

FaceTime configuration for phone conversations. Navigate to Settings > Phone on the iPhone (iOS 9 or later) as well as enable Wi-Fi calling. Launch FaceTime on your Mac thereafter. Select "General" from the Settings menu, then tap "Calls from iPhone".

Communicate via FaceTime and Messages. Sending and receiving text messages from the MacBook Air, utilize Messages. You can respond to a text message using the closest available gadget from the MacBook Air, iPhone, iPad, iPod touch, as well as

Apple Watch, as all messages are displayed on these devices.

Implement Effects In A Videoconference

Utilizing a compatible camera and a video-captaining application, such as FaceTime, you can supplement your videoconferencing experience with a variety of video effects.

The functionality of specific video effects may be limited to the Mac model or the iPhone that is being utilized as the webcam.

A Zoom meeting in which the Video interface is active.

Strengthen your video. Make adjustments to the illumination, background blur, and other video parameters. Select an option corresponding to your camera, including Portrait, Centre Stage, or Studio Light, by clicking the Video symbol within the menu bar.

Respond to the discourse. Incorporate 3D effects that adorn the camera frame, such as pyrotechnics, hearts, debris, and more, into a reaction. Select a reaction by clicking the Video symbol within the menu bar, followed by the menu next to Reactions. A reaction can also be expressed through the use of a hand gesture. a comprehensive inventory of available hand gestures for responding can be found within the FaceTime User Guide.

Select the screen you wish to share with ease.
During a FaceTime or additional supported videoconferencing application session, it is simple to share a single app or several apps directly from the window. While hovering the mouse over the Mission Control icon located in the upper-left corner of the window, select Share on [the name of your videoconferencing application].

You may superimpose your video on the shared display. Choose between large as well as tiny overlays. With your screen framed adjacent to you on a separate layer, the large overlay maintains the focus on you. In contrast, the small overlay renders you in a movable sphere above the shared display. Select the Video symbol within the menu bar, then select Presenter Overlay Size (Large or Small).

Experiences Can Be Shared Via Shareplay
SharePlay enables you and your family and friends to view content, listen to music, and watch television and movies together. Your companions may utilize an iPhone (iOS 15 or later), iPad (iPadOS 15 or later),

or Mac running macOS Monterey or later to participate. Additionally, content can be viewed on Apple TV (tvOS 15 or later) whilst conversing with peers on another device.

Note: Participation in certain SharePlay-compatible applications requires a paid subscription. In some regions as well as countries, access to particular content and features is restricted.

The FaceTime interface displays a call in which all participants are listening to the same album via SharePlay.

Commence using FaceTime. Commence FaceTime conversation, extend invitations to acquaintances, relatives, or coworkers, and subsequently employ the SharePlay icon to impart an experience to them. Additionally, SharePlay link can be appended to a Message thread.

Attend the show together. Incorporate a variety of media, including movies, television programs, and web videos, into your FaceTime group conversations and bond with others while you watch videos. While pausing, rewinding, fast-forwarding, or skipping to a different scene, the playback of all participants remains in sync. Intelligent volume automatically adjusts the intensity, allowing you to continue conversing while viewing.

Listen in unison. During FaceTime conversations, you and your peers can share music or organize a massive dance celebration. Any participant in the call may add tracks to the shared roster while hearing in concert. All participants in the call have access to the playback controls, and by employing sensible volume while listening, all members can engage in conversation without resorting to shouting.

Display your screen to others. Utilize SharePlay to incorporate websites, applications, and other things into your FaceTime conversation. The user can include anything that is displayed on their screen in a shared moment. Collaboratively peruse vacation rentals, procure bridesmaid gowns, impart a novel skill, or present an unplanned slideshow in Photos. You have the option of sharing a single window or the entire screen.

CAPTURE A SCREENSHOT USING YOUR MAC

By navigating to the Screenshot menu, one can locate every control required to capture screen recordings and screenshots. Additionally, your voice can be captured during a screen recording. The optimized workflow enables you to capture and edit videos and photos of your screen, as well as save, share, and modify them with ease.

Navigate to the screenshot settings. Hold down Command-Shift-5. The entire screen, a selected window, or a portion of a window can be captured. Additionally, the entire screen or a specified portion of the screen can be recorded.

Utilize the icons located at the bottom of the display to document your screen (document Screen icon ⌐⌐), capture a selection (Capture Screen Selection symbol ⬛), and more. To modify the saved location, set a timer before capturing, configure the microphone as well as audio, or display the pointer, select Options. Select Capture or Record to capture a video or screenshot.

Following the capture of a video or screenshot, a miniature is displayed in one quadrant of the display. To rapidly save the thumbnail to a document or folder, drag it in; to alter or share it, slide to the right, or click.

Additionally, the Screenshot utility can be accessed via the Other folder within Launchpad or the Applications > Utilities folder within the Finder.

Annotate the screenshot with text. Select the thumbnail of your screenshot to annotate it using markup tools. Additionally, you have the option to share your annotated screen with colleagues or acquaintances by clicking the Share symbol⬆ directly from the screenshot.

A screenshot that has been annotated with red changes and corrections.

BACK UP AND RESTORE YOUR MAC

It is critical to routinely create backups of your MacBook Air to protect your files. The built-in Time Machine on your Mac enables you to create backups of your documents, applications, accounts, settings, music, photographs, as well as videos. Time Machine does not perform backups of the macOS platform.

Choose a location for the backup of your files. External storage gadgets that are linked to the MacBook Air, in addition to other supported storage devices, can be backed up using Time Machine."

Establish a time machine. Consult the accompanying documentation for your storage device before commencing. Ensure that your MacBook Air is connected to the same Wi-Fi network as the external storage device, or link the two devices using a cable and, if necessary, an adapter. Select General > Time Machine from the System Preferences menu, followed by Add Backup Disc. After selecting the drive to be used for backups, you are ready to proceed.

Back up your files. You can restore your files using Time Machine, and you can choose to restore specific files or all of them at once. Select the Time Machine symbol ⟳ from the menu bar, then select "Browse Time Machine backups." From there, select one or more objects (folders or the entire disc) that you wish to restore, and then select Restore.

Note: To locate the Time Machine symbol within the sidebar, select Control Centre from the Apple Menu > System Settings. Right-click the pop-up menu adjacent to Time Machine and select Show in the Menu Bar.

Reinstall macOS. A sealed system disc is utilized to separate your operating system files from your files. Certain operations, such as eradicating or accidentally damaging a disc, do, however, necessitate a system restore on your MacBook Air. It is possible to reinstall macOS and subsequently retrieve personal files from a backup using Time Machine. Since macOS Big Sur as well as later, restoring your Mac can be accomplished in a variety of methods. You might be obligated to install a macOS version more recent than the one that was pre-damaged on your computer or the one that was initially installed.

Advanced users must generate a bootable installer to reinstall macOS at a later time. This may be advantageous if you wish to utilize a particular version of macOS.

CONTENT SHARING ACROSS DEVICES

Multiple methods exist for transferring content among Apple gadgets. Utilize AirDrop to share files, photos, as well as credentials, and utilize Universal Clipboard for copying and pasting between gadgets.

FILE AND OTHER SHARING VIA AIRDROP

A Finder window in which AirDrop is enabled within the sidebar's Favourites section.

Sharing files with adjacent Mac, iPod, and iPhone touch gadgets is simplified with AirDrop. It is not required that both gadgets utilize the same Apple ID.

Activate AirDrop. Select AirDrop by clicking the Control Centre icon in the menu bar, followed by the AirDrop icon. Choose "Contacts only" or "Everyone" to regulate the recipients of AirDrop content.

Transfer a file using the Finder. Control-click the item you wish to transmit, select Share > AirDrop, and then choose the recipient device. Alternately, select AirDrop from the sidebar on the left after clicking the Finder icon in the Dock (or by selecting Go > AirDrop). When the recipient of the file shows up in the window, transfer it to them by dragging it from the desktop or another Finder window. Upon transmission of a file, the recipient is granted the option of accepting or declining the file.

Transmit a file using an app. Select the Share icon and select AirDrop whilst using an application such as Pages or Preview. Then, select the device to which you wish to deliver the item.

If the recipient is not visible in the AirDrop window, ensure that both devices are within 30 feet (9 meters) of one another with AirDrop and Bluetooth enabled. Attempt to locate the intended recipient using a older Mac by selecting "Don't see who you're searching for?"

Deliver products through AirDrop. When an item is sent to you via AirDrop on your Mac, you are presented with the option of accepting and conserving it. Click Accept when you receive the AirDrop notification as well as decide to keep the item in an application such as Photos or your Downloads folder. By utilizing the same iCloud account across multiple devices, it becomes effortless to transfer an item (such as an iPhone photo) from one gadget to another, with the added benefit that the transfer is automatically preserved.

Implement Handoff On A Mac

Click to continue what you were doing on your iPhone.

The Dock icon represents the Handoff.

Handoff enables the continuation of an activity from one device to another. Commence a FaceTime conversation using your iPhone, and upon returning to your desk, transmit the connection to your MacBook Air. Alternatively, you may commence a presentation on the iPad while working on a MacBook Air. Observe and respond to messages from your Apple Watch and MacBook Air, respectively. Pages, FaceTime, Safari, Mail, Calendar, Contacts,

Maps, Notes, Reminders, Messages, Keynote, as well as Pages are all compatible with Handoff.

Transferring operations between gadgets. While your MacBook Air along with additional gadgets are nearby, a symbol appears within the Dock for the majority of activities that can be delegated. By clicking the symbol, you can switch between gadgets.

There is no handoff icon in the Dock for FaceTime. To transfer a call from your iPad or iPhone to the MacBook Air, select the video icon ⬚ from the Mac's menu bar, and then choose Switch, followed by Join within the FaceTime window. To transfer a FaceTime call from the MacBook Air to your iPad or iPhone, touch the video symbol ⬚, followed by tapping Switch twice on the device's upper left corner.

Enable the Handoff feature on the MacBook Air. In the sidebar of System Preferences, navigate to General > Airdrop & Handoff > Airdrop & Handoff > "Allow Handoff between this Mac as well as your iCloud gadgets."

Enable the Handoff feature on your iOS or iPad gadget. Tap Handoff from the Settings > General > Handoff menu to enable it. If the Handoff option is not visible, the device in question does not support it.

Activate the Handoff feature on the Apple Watch. To enable handoff, navigate to Settings > General within the Apple Watch application on your iPhone, and then select.

COPYING AND PASTING ACROSS DEVICES

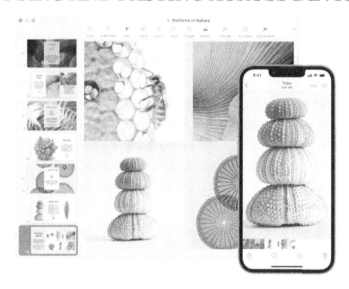

An iPhone displays a photograph alongside a Mac displaying the same image after it has been inserted into a Pages document.

Rapidly copy content from one adjacent device and transfer it to another device nearby. All Mac, iPad, iPhone, and iPod touch gadgets that have been signed in using the identical Apple ID and that are Handoff, Wi-Fi, as well as Bluetooth enabled receive the contents of your clipboard via Wi-Fi.

Pasting and copying files. Transferring files between Macs is a straightforward process with the Universal Clipboard. Paste a file that supports copying and pasting from an adjacent app onto a

Finder window, Mail message, or any other application on the MacBook Air. On both computers, you must be logged in with the identical Apple ID.

Utilize Your iPhone to Capture Images On Your Mac

An iPhone displays a photograph and a Mac displays a Pages document alongside an input field specifying the location of the photograph.

By enabling Continuity Camera on your Mac, you can utilize your iPhone as an additional camera. You can capture images with the camera on your iPhone to save them to a Mac or incorporate them into your documents.

Incorporate a scan or image. Utilize the camera capabilities of your iPod touch, iPhone, or iPad to capture images of adjacent objects or to scan documents. Immediately, the image is displayed on your Mac. Select the destination for the image in an application such as Mail, Notes, or Messages; then select File (or Insert) > Import From iPhone or iPad; select Take Photo or Scan Documents; as well as finally, capture the image using an iOS or iPadOS gadget. Select Continue Scan or Use Photo. You may also select Retake to attempt the task once more.

Select the desired location for the image in an application such as Pages, then control-click, select "Import image," as well as capture the image. It may be necessary to choose the gadget before capturing the image.

Note: To capture a scan on an iOS or iPadOS gadget, drag the frame till the desired content is visible, and then press Save after selecting Keep Scan. To rescan the content, select Retake.

The image or scan is positioned in the desired location within the document.

AIRPLAY ALLOWS YOU TO STREAM MATERIAL ON A LARGER DISPLAY

A MacBook Air with an Apple TV mirroring its content onto a large, high-definition television.

Stream content from your MacBook Air to the large screen via AirPlay, or transfer content to the Mac from an iPhone, iPad, or another Mac. Mirroring the MacBook Air display onto a high-definition television is possible, as is using the television as a secondary display. Connect your MacBook Air to Apple TV and ensure that Apple TV is connected to the same Wi-Fi network as your device. Additionally, you can play web videos directly on your high-definition television without displaying your desktop, which is useful i you want to watch a movie while keeping your work private.

Transfer files to your Mac from external devices. Observe videos, listen to audio, and perform other tasks while they are being played o other devices, all on your Mac. Apply an extended display to your Mac by mirroring your iPhone or iPad onto it, or by utilizing applications that support it including Keynote as well as Photos, to extend the display on your Mac. Utilize your Mac as a secondary speaker for multiroom audio or as an AirPlay speaker for streaming music or podcasts to it. Your Mac is compatible with all Apple devices, and sharing an Apple ID makes the connection even simpler.

Use Screen Mirroring to replicate your desktop. To enable AirPlay on your Apple TV, select Screen Mirroring⬜ from the Control Centre symbol 🎚 in the menu bar. Once AirPlay is enabled, the symbol will change color to blue.

Note: If the Mac enables AirPlay screen mirroring, while an Apple TV is connected to the same network as your Mac, an AirPlay status symbol will appear within the menu bar.

Stream online videos while concealing your desktop. Once you locate a web video that features an AirPlay indicator⬚, choose your Apple TV by clicking the icon.

Apple Stores and Apple.com offer Apple TV for purchase separately.

If the mirrored image does not suit the screen of your high-definition television, modify the scale of your desktop for the clearest image. Select a button under Match Desktop Size To after clicking the AirPlay symbol⬚ within the video.

CHAPTER SIX

OPERATE YOUR MACBOOK AIR WITH OTHER DEVICES

Your Mac is compatible with all other Apple products. Continuity enables the simultaneous use of an Apple Watch, Mac, iPad, or iPhone to access potent features.

Before embarking. Ensure that both your iOS or iPadOS gadget as well as the MacBook Air you're using have Bluetooth and Wi-Fi enabled and that you are signed in using the same Apple ID.

EMPLOY AN IPHONE ON A MAC

A MacBook Air displaying a FaceTime session with the Continuity Camera on Centre Stage.

Implement iPhone applications on the desktop. Import your iPhone applications into the desktop of your Mac. To transfer iPhone widgets to your Mac, utilize the Widget Gallery or drag widgets from the Notification Centre to your desktop. To access the Widget Gallery, select Edit Widgets after performing a control-click on the desktop.

Employ the iPhone's webcam feature. By enabling Continuity Camera on your Mac, you can utilize your iPhone as an additional camera. The iPhone's camera is capable of facilitating video conversations. Continuity Camera enables your Mac to seamlessly transition to using your iPhone as a camera while it is within range, following its configuration. Alternatively, a wired connection is also an option. See in the macOS User Guide, "Choose an external camera" and "Utilize your iPhone as a webcam."

For the Continuity Camera to function as a webcam, an iPhone XR or later is required. To share photos via Continuity Camera, the following devices are required: an iPhone or iPod touch running iOS 12 or later, or an iPad with iPadOS 13.1 or later installed.

Employ the iPhone's microphone. Continuity Camera enables the iPhone to function as a Mac microphone. FaceTime users can select their iPhone during a call using the Video menu, while video conversations can be switched to the iPhone's microphone via app settings. You can also designate your iPhone as the system microphone via the Audio settings in System Preferences.

Utilize iPhone applications on a Mac. Your preferred iPhone and iPad applications are compatible with your Mac.

Text communications and phone calls on a Mac. Calls can be made and received directly from the MacBook Air via a Wi-Fi connection. Additionally, both sending and receiving text messages are possible.

Navigate to Settings > Phone on your iPhone as well as enable Wi-Fi calling. Launch FaceTime on your Mac thereafter. Go to Settings, select General, and then pick "Calls from iPhone."

Implement an iPhone hotspot. Have you lost Wi-Fi connectivity? Instant Hotspot enables you to link your MacBook Air to the internet immediately through the Personal Hotspot on the iPhone or iPad—no password required.

To view the list of available networks on your iPhone or iPad, select the Links icon next to it from the Wi-Fi status icon in the menu bar. If the list does not appear, select Other Networks. The Wi-Fi indicator is replaced with the Links icon in the toolbar. There is no action required on your part; the MacBook Air automatically connects. To conserve battery life, the MacBook Air disconnects from the hotspot when it is not in use.

If prompted for a password, verify that your devices are properly configured. See the article from Apple Support. Connect to your Hotspot without inputting a password using Instant Hotspot.

EMPLOY AN IPAD ALONGSIDE A MAC

An iPad and a MacBook Air are positioned side by side. The artwork is displayed in the Illustrator navigator window on the MacBook Air. The iPad displays the identical artwork within the Illustrator document window, which is enclosed by toolbars.

Maximize the performance of your MacBook Air by connecting it to your iPad. Sidecar enables the utilization of the iPad as an additional display for the Mac, providing additional workspace to spread out tasks and utilize the Apple Pencil to draw within preferred Mac applications. Using Universal Control, it is also possible to manipulate content between iPadOS as well as macOS by connecting your iPad to the Mac via its keyboard, mouse, or trackpad. Additionally, you can annotate PDFs, screenshots, and much more rapidly.

Employ the iPad as an additional display for the Mac. Sidecar enables you to maintain the iPad's charge while using it wirelessly within ten meters (32 feet) of your Mac, or by connecting it to your Mac via cable. Select the iPad's display from the Add Display pop-up menu after navigating to Apple > System Settings > Displays. This will enable you to configure your iPad as a secondary display. You can later establish a connection to your iPad via the Control Center's Display section . To detach the iPad from your Mac, select Sidecar from the Control Centre menu. Additionally, the Disconnect icon can be found in the sidebar of the iPad.

iPad models that can use the Apple Pencil and operate iPadOS 13.1 (or later) are compatible with Sidecar.

Configure Sidecar options. Launch System Preferences, navigate to Displays, and then select the iPad's name. Then, you can configure Sidecar settings regarding your iPad, including whether it serves as the primary display or merely a mirror of your Mac, whether the sidebar is visible and its location, and whether the Apple Pencil can be used to access tools with a double-click.

If your iPad has not yet been configured, these options will be hidden in the Display settings.

Employ a Mac Pencil. Precisely construct and draw using your preferred professional applications. Simply transfer the window from your Mac to your iPad to begin utilizing the Apple Pencil. Apple Pencil can also be utilized to annotate PDFs, screenshots, as well as images.

Pressure and tilt support for the Apple Pencil is limited to applications that support sophisticated styluses.

Mirror or extend your interface. Upon connection, the iPad becomes an extension of the Mac desktop, enabling the seamless dragging of applications and documents between the two devices. To mirror the display and have your Mac screen appear on both devices, hover your mouse above the Sidecar icon. To access the Sidecar menu option in the Control Centre, hover over the icon and choose Mirror Built-in Retina Display with the right arrow that appears. To extend your desktop once more, click Use As Separate Display from the menu.

Maximize the use of auxiliary shortcuts. Utilize the iPad's sidebar to access frequently used icons and controls rapidly. To display or conceal the menu bar, Dock, as well as the keyboard, utilize keyboard shortcuts or restore previous actions, and tap the corresponding controls.

To ensure convenient access to the Sidecar choices, it is possible to configure the Display settings to consistently manifest in the menu bar. Navigate to System Settings > Control Centre, then select whether the Displays symbol should always appear in the menu bar or only when active via the pop-up menu next to Displays. The Sidecar menu option replaces the Display symbol within the menu bar when Sidecar  is enabled and the iPad is connected.

Placing a MacBook Air and an iPad side by side. The iPad screen displays an annotated leaflet. The attachment to the email message displayed on the MacBook Air is the annotated flyer that was created on the iPad.

One keypad, mouse, or trackpad may be utilized to operate multiple devices. With Universal Control, you can control various gadgets using a single keyboard, mouse, or trackpad. You can collaborate on up to three devices simultaneously by transferring the pointer to an iPad or a different Mac when you approach the perimeter of the display on your MacBook Air.

It is necessary to have iPadOS 15.4 or later on your iPad as well as macOS 12.3 or later on your Mac to utilize Universal Control.

Verify all connections. Universal Control on your Mac detects as well as connects to other devices via Wi-Fi and Bluetooth, respectively. Ensure that Bluetooth is enabled and that each device is connected to Wi-Fi. Additionally, ensure that Handoff is enabled in Settings > General > AirPlay and Handoff on your iPad as well as within the General settings of your MacBook Air. Additionally, both gadgets must be logged in with the identical Apple ID as well as two-factor authorization must be enabled. While these parameters are accurate, you can link gadgets using Control Centre. In the menu bar of Control Centre on your Mac, select Screen Mirroring, followed by the gadget listed beneath Link Keyboard as well as Mouse.

Navigate between displays. Utilize the mouse or trackpad on your Mac to position the pointer to the screen's right or left edge in closest proximity to the iPad. After pausing, faintly advance the pointer beyond the screen's edge. Proceed with navigating the iPad screen in the presence of a border that appears at the screen's perimeter.

Utilize drag-and-drop. After selecting the object to be moved, such as text, an image, or another element, drag it to the desired location on the other gadget. For instance, an Apple Pencil design created on an iPad can be dragged and dropped into the Keynote application running on a MacBook Air.

Additionally, something that is copied on one device can be pasted on the other.

Collaborate on a keyboard. Start entering characters when the insertion point is flickering within a document or another area where text can be entered.

CHAPTER SEVEN

APPLICATIONS ON YOUR MACBOOK AIR

 PHOTOS

Organize, edit, and share pictures and videos using Photos and iCloud Photos, while maintaining an up-to-date photo library across every one of your gadgets. Photos exhibit your finest photographs, and enhanced search capabilities make it effortless to locate and appreciate your favorites. Using intuitive editing tools, you can modify your photographs and videos with ease. Moreover, with iCloud Shared Photo Library, you and up to five others can collaborate on an album by adding and organizing pictures and videos, leaving comments, and admiring one another's modifications.

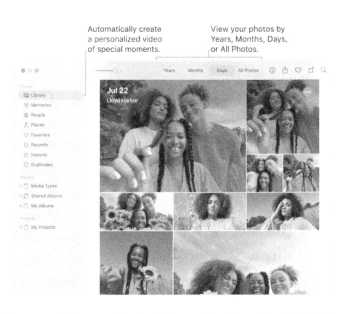

Automatically create a personalized video of special moments.

View your photos by Years, Months, Days, or All Photos.

The Photos window with the Memories function is displayed in the left sidebar as well as the album's photos sortable by day, month, and year via a pop-up menu at the highest point of the Photos window.

Every single one of your gadgets' photos. You can search, browse, and share photos and video from all of your gadgets that are signed in with the same Apple ID using iCloud Photos. A photo captured with an iPhone is displayed instantaneously on all of your other devices. Additionally, any modifications you make to photos are reflected across all of your gadgets. Launch System Preferences, select your Apple ID from the sidebar, then click iCloud, followed by the Photos option.

Create a shared photo library in iCloud. By maintaining a separate library for photos and videos the entire family can reminisce in greater detail. The user's content and content from the Shared Library are seamlessly merged within the Photos application

When an individual uploads or modifies a photo or video in the Shared Library, the modifications are visible to all library members. Participation is permitted in a single communal library with a maximum of five other individuals.

iCloud Photos must be enabled while you must be signed in using your Apple ID to configure iCloud Shared Photo Library. Select Get Started from the Shared Library tab within the Photos > Settings menu. You have the option of adding participants immediately or at a later time. Choose which of your previous photos and videos to add to the Shared Library: an archive of every photo and video, those featuring specific individuals or captured after a particular date, or manually select desired photos and videos. Once the Shared Library has been established, you can switch between your Library, the Shared Library, or both simultaneously in Photos.

Videos and images can be added to the Shared Library. To transfer specific photographs or videos to the Shared Library, perform the following action: Control-click the photo or video within your Library and select "Move to Shared Library." Additionally, to obtain recommendations for photos or videos that you might like to include, navigate to Photos > Settings, select the Shared Library tab, and then select "Add People" from the Shared Library Suggestions menu.

Conveyed to You. When photographs are forwarded to you via Messages from friends in your Contacts, they are promptly displayed in the Shared with You section of your photographs application. Your library contains photographs that you are most likely to see and enjoy, such as those from events you have attended. You can initiate a new conversation by clicking the message icon on a photo while examining it in the Photos application.

Edit with expertise. Produce exceptional photographs and videos by utilizing robust yet user-friendly editing tools. Simply by clicking the editing icons located above your image or video, you can enhance it. To access more robust editing tools, select Edit and then employ Smart Sliders to achieve polished outcomes. It is possible to apply filters, rotate, enhance exposure, and crop videos as well as photographs.

Communicate using text. Live Text can identify text within images found on the web and on your computer. You can copy text from an image to transfer into any file on your Mac, or you can access a website or phone number by clicking on it to access the site or dial the number, respectively. Select the text you wish to translate, then Control-click it before clicking Translate. Languages other than those specified are unavailable.

Relive moments of significance. Significant events such as vacations, birthdays, and anniversaries are highlighted in photographs. Live Photos and videos are incorporated into your photo library to animate it as you browse. By selecting Memories from the sidebar, Photos will generate a customizable and shareable movie that is rich in music, titles, transitions, moods, and more. Your Memories are accessible from any of your other iCloud Photos-enabled devices.

Identify the item that you are seeking. By showcasing the finest images in your library, Photos conceals invoices, duplicates, and screenshots. To view your entire collection at a glance, select All Photos or the icons located at the top of the Photos window labeled "Year," "Month," or "Day." Photos enable users to search their photos and videos by identifying objects, settings, and people within them, as well as by the date of capture, individuals mentioned in the photos, captions added, and the locations of the subjects, if available. Additionally, Spotlight and Siri can be utilized to seek photos.

Query Siri. Propose the following: "Present me with photographs featuring Ursula."

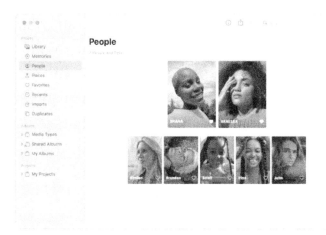

Individuals' albums within the Photos interface.

Places, individuals, and objects. Visual Lookup identifies a multitude of objects within your photographs. To emphasize identifiable locations and objects, swipe upwards on an image or select the information icon. Gain a deeper understanding of well-known works of art and international landmarks, flora and blossoms, literature, and companion varieties. To ensure that photos of significant others are consistently showcased at the highest position of the People album, select the Favourites icon♡ that is displayed next to their image. Utilize the Places album to generate an interactive map from all of your photographs that contain location data. By zooming in on the map, additional images from a particular location become visible.

Location data can be added to any photograph. Click the Information icon(i), then select Assign a

Location, and begin typing while viewing the image. Enter the destination followed by the Return key, or select the location from the list.

Inspire your imagination with Live Photos. Utilize the Loop effect to iterate the action continuously in Live Photos, or the Bounce effect to perform the animation in both forward and reverse motion. Utilize Long Exposure to obscure motion within your Live Photos as well as elevate an ordinary waterfall or streaming stream to the status of a work of art for a professional DSLR appearance.

 **APP STORE**

Utilize the App Store to locate and acquire applications, as well as to obtain the most recent enhancements for your existing apps.

Discover the ideal app. Do you know precisely what you are seeking? After entering the name of the application into the search field, select Return. Applications acquired from the App Store are promptly installed in Launchpad. Alternatively, you can discover new applications by selecting an auxiliary tab—for instance, Create, Work, or Play—and perusing the outcomes.

Click a tab to browse apps.

Search for an app by name.

A page of Safari Extensions and the search field are displayed within the App Store window.

Apple Arcade is not universally accessible across all regions or countries.

Query Siri. Use the phrase "Find apps for children."

An Apple ID is all that is required. Sign in with the Apple ID you use to obtain free applications by clicking Sign In at the bottom of the App Store sidebar. To create an Apple ID if you do not already have one, select Sign In followed by Create Apple ID. To retrieve an Apple ID password that you have forgotten, select "Forgot Apple ID or password?" Additionally, you must create an account with your payment information to acquire fee-based applications.

Utilize applications for the iPhone and iPad on a Mac. Numerous applications for the iPhone and iPad are compatible with the MacBook Air. Applications that were previously acquired for the iPhone or iPad are displayed on the Mac. Perform a search for applications within the App Store to determine whether or not they are compatible with Mac.

The game has begun. To learn how to subscribe to Apple Arcade, uncover games that are available for play, identify games that are popular among your Game Centre peers, track your achievement progress, and more, navigate to the Arcade tab. Downloaded games from the App Store are automatically categorized in the Games subdirectory in Launchpad, ensuring convenient accessibility even when using a game controller.

Game Mode is engaged. Game Mode automatically assigns games the highest priority on the CPU as well as the GPU of your Mac while it is in use, thereby reducing resource utilization for secondary duties. Furthermore, it effectively diminishes latency when utilizing wireless accessories such as AirPods as well as preferred controllers, resulting in a tangible sense of responsiveness.

Preserve your in-game progress. On supported third-party game controllers, you can capture and archive a 15-second video recording of gameplay by selecting the share icon. This feature allows you to retrospectively analyze your game strategy or preserve noteworthy moments from your gaming experience.

Gather your companions for a game. Adding groups and friends from recent Messages with ease to multiplayer friend selectors that are compatible with Game Centre is a simple feature update. Observe invitations as well as incoming requests within the friend request inbox.

Obtain the most recent app updates. The presence of a badge on the App Store symbol within the Dock indicates the availability of updates. To access the App Store, select the symbol, and then select Updates from the sidebar.

A segment of the Dock that displays the badged App Store symbol, signifying the presence of available updates.

5 THE CALENDAR

Calendar ensures that no appointment is missed. Organize and monitor your hectic schedule by establishing multiple calendars in a single location.

Establish programs. Double-tap anywhere within a day to add a new event by selecting the Add icon ✛. Spotlight can also be utilized to rapidly introduce a new event. Double-click the event, navigate to the Add Invitees section, and enter an email address to invite a participant. You are notified via calendar when your invitees respond.

Query Siri. Propose the following: "Organize a meeting with Mark for 9:00 a.m."

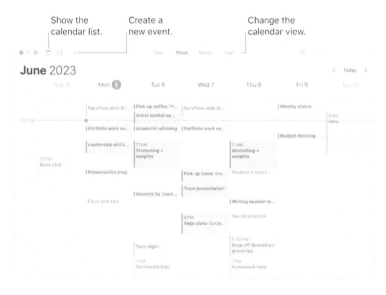

A Calendar window that displays the event roster, the method for creating events, and the options to select the Day, Week, Month, or Year view.

When a location is added to an event, the Calendar provides additional information such as a map, estimated travel time as well as departure time, and weather forecast.

An all-encompassing calendar for one's existence. Create color-coded calendars for distinct purposes, such as home, work, and school. To create a calendar, select File > New Calendar, and subsequently Command-click each calendar to modify its color.

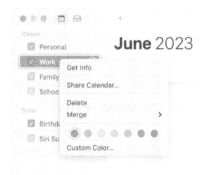

A calendar auxiliary menu containing color customization options.

Include holiday schedules. Peruse holiday calendars originating from various global regions. Select File > New Holiday Calendar, followed by the desired holiday calendar.

Observe your entire calendar or a select few. A list of your calendars can be accessed by clicking the Calendars icon; select the ones you wish to view in the window.

Implement calendar filters with Focus. Determine which calendars will be displayed during a specific Focus. Consider utilizing a calendar that displays assignment due dates exclusively during periods of study. After selecting Apple Menu > System Preferences, select Focus from the sidebar. Select a focus on the right, then select Add Filter under Focus Filters by clicking the right arrow.

Sharing is possible with others and across devices. iCloud ensures that your calendars remain current across all of your Apple Watch, Macintosh computers, iOS-based gadgets, iPadOS gadgets, as well as gadgets that are also signed in with the identical Apple ID. Additionally, calendars can be shared among other iCloud users.

SAFARI

Safari is a robust and streamlined web browser that incorporates cutting-edge privacy measures, such as passkeys. Safari remains consistent across Mac, iPhone, as well as iPad devices, ensuring that users access the same interface regardless of the device they are on, provided they maintain an active iCloud subscription with an identical Apple ID.

Set out your quest. When you begin inputting a word or website address into Safari, it displays both recommended and matching websites. In addition, you may choose a frequently visited or favored item from the Safari home screen. To initiate a new search in a new tab, press Command-T or select the Add icon + in the far right corner of the Safari window.

A restricted Safari window that features an indication of the search field in the upper-right corner.

Select the Reader symbol located to the left of the search bar to access pages in Reader mode, where advertisements and other distractions are eliminated. Select the Font symbol AA while in Reader mode to modify the font and color.

Quickly view the contents of a tab. On tabs, favicons—icons or emblems that are affiliated with a website—enable quick identification of a particular page. By hovering the cursor over a tab, a preview of the page's content can be viewed.

Consult the sidebar. Tab Groups, bookmarks, the Reading List, as well as Shared with You URLs are displayed in the sidebar. To access the sidebar links, select the icon □ that appears. To view all the tab contained within a group, you may also expand Tab Groups by selecting the Tab pop-up menu ⌄ located adjacent to Tab Groups within the sidebar.

The current profile; click to open a window in a different profile.

A Safari window that is embedded within the School profile.

Maintain a distinct browsing history for profiles. Establish distinct profiles in Safari, such a

"School" and "Personal," to maintain the segregation of your history, favorites, Tab Groups, and other components. Select New Profile from the Create Profile menu in Safari, then input a name and customize the profile with a color, symbol, and additional options. To create another profile after creating an existing one, select the Add icon $+$.

For immediate translation of available webpages in Safari, when the translate button shows up in the website address field, select it. The availability of translation features varies across regions and languages. Safari provides an inventory of the languages that are supported: Web Page Translation.

Implement organization using tab groups. You may create a Tab Group for websites that you wish to retain together while investigating a project or vacation. To proceed with the creation of a group from the currently open windows, select New Tab Group from the Add Tab Group symbol that appears in the sidebar. To combine some of the tabs you have opened into a new Tab Group, hold down the Command key, then select the Add Tab Group symbol next to each tab you wish to include in the group.

By extending an invitation to collaborate on a Tab Group through Messages, all participants are inadvertently included as members of the Tab Group.

Select the More Options symbol adjacent to the Tab Group you wish to share in the sidebar, then select Share Tab Group, followed by Messages. While in a Tab Group that you have shared, collaborators can add their tabs and you can view the page that others are presently viewing.

It is important to mention that Tab Groups are accessible from any location on an iCloud-enabled gadget using the same Apple ID.

Investigate extension programs. Extensions augment Safari with features that allow you to customize your browsing experience. Extensions that block advertisements, locate coupons, correct your grammar, and rapidly save content from your favorite websites are available. To access the App Store's extensions category, select Safari > Safari Extensions. This section showcases featured Safari extensions and categories, including Browse Better, Read with Ease, Top Free Apps, as well as more. Once extensions have been obtained, enable them in the Safari settings. To activate extensions, navigate to the Extensions tab and select the appropriate entries.

Web app appears
in the Dock.

A web application in the Dock with its icon visible.

Convert your preferred websites into web applications. By adding a website to the Dock, users can conveniently access and monitor website notifications. Open the site in Safari, then select Add to Dock from the Share menu ⬆️ that appears by the right arrow within the far right corner of the window to develop a web application. After entering a name, select Add.

Obtain merchandise by utilizing Apple Pay. Employing Apple Pay on the MacBook Air, you can make private, secure, and effortless online purchases through Safari. When selecting Apple Pay on a website, gently touch the Touch ID sensor located on the MacBook Air. Additionally, you may utilize the iPhone or Apple Watch to verify payment.

Apple Pay ensures that no debit or credit card data associated with your Apple Card is stored or disclosed by Apple to the.

Apple Pay as well as Apple Card are not universally accessible across all countries and regions. To learn more about Apple Pay, please visit Apple Pay.

Passphrases safeguard your data. Passkeys ensure your security when using Touch ID or Face ID to log in to websites instead of a password. Additionally, passkeys function on non-Apple devices. Passkeys are even more secure than two-factor authentication because they safeguard against fraud and information breaches. They are stored in the iCloud keychain. Additionally, passkeys can be shared with a group of contacts.

To utilize passkeys, the Password & Keychain option must be enabled in Cloud Settings. When logging into a website, select the option to store its passkey. You may utilize Touch ID or your iPhone or iPad to log in.

Surf the Internet securely. Safari notifies you when you encounter an insecure website that potentially attempts to deceive you into divulging sensitive information. Additionally, Safari safeguards against web surveillance and prevents fingerprinting from being used to identify your Mac. Intelligent Tracking Prevention combats cross-site tracking by identifying as well as eradicating the data that trackers leave behind, utilizing the most recent advancements in machine learning as well as on-device intelligence.

Practice seclusion. To generate a private browsing window, select File > New Private Window from the menu. Your private window becomes locked when it is not in use, requiring the login process or Touch ID to enable it. Safari does not retain your browsing history, aids in thwarting website tracking, prevents known trackers from launching entirely on pages, and eliminates tracking employed to ascertain your identity from URLs while you browse.

Select the Privacy Report icon⬚ to the left of the active tab to access the cross-site trackers that Safari is blocking on every website, thereby enhancing your understanding of how a site handles your privacy. By selecting the Full Report optionⓘ, a privacy report containing additional information regarding the website's active trackers will be displayed.

Your email address should be concealed. With an iCloud+ subscription, you can generate an infinite number of unique, arbitrary email addresses at any time (for instance, when filling out a form on a website). Any email that is sent to the Hide My Email address that you specify for a website is forwarded to your email account. A Hide My Email address allows you to receive emails without disclosing your actual address, and it can be deactivated at any time.

 FACETIME

FaceTime enables you to make audio and video conversations with a friend or group of acquaintances from your Mac. FaceTime also enables you to utilize your iPhone or iPad in novel ways with your MacBook Air, such as by transferring conversations between gadgets or by employing the iPhone camera as a webcam.

Query Siri. Say something along the lines of "Call Sharon via FaceTime."

Apply FaceTime to a communication. FaceTime HD video conversations can be initiated using the Mac's integrated camera. FaceTime after entering the name, phone number, or email address of the recipient into the New FaceTime field. To make an audio-only call when video calls are inconvenient, select FaceTime Audio from the pop-up menu. Upon receiving a FaceTime invitation, the option to participate via audio or video is presented.

You can transfer the small picture-in-picture window onto any corner of the FaceTime window while video call is in session.

List of recent calls

A FaceTime window containing a catalog of recent calls and icons to establish a link for a FaceTime connection or to initiate a new FaceTime contact.

Convey a FaceTime conversation. Commence a FaceTime conversation on your iPhone while you are away from home, then transfer the contact to your Mac upon your return to your workstation. Conversely, you may accept FaceTime calls from your Mac while transferring to another device as necessary. If Bluetooth headphones are connected, they also perform the transition.

To transfer a FaceTime call from your iPad or iPhone to the MacBook Air, in the FaceTime window on the MacBook Air, select Join after selecting the video symbol⬜◁ within the menu bar on the Mac. To transfer a FaceTime call from the MacBook Air to the iPad or iPhone, touch the video symbol⬜◁, followed by tapping Switch twice on the device's upper left corner.

A FaceTime conversation between an iPhone and a Mac desktop with Keynote open. To transition a FaceTime call to the Mac, press the icon located in the upper-right quadrant of the device.

Employ the iPhone's webcam feature. Utilize the capabilities of the iPhone camera to conduct FaceTime sessions on your Mac. Place your iPhone in a stand or other stable, landscape orientation position, with the rear cameras facing you and, the screen off. Navigate to FaceTime > Video on your Mac, then choose the device you are using from the list. The Ultra Wide camera on iPhone 11 later enables Centre Stage, whereby the communication remains centered on the subject while the subject moves. By selecting the Video icon ◼️ from the menu bar, you can access additional video effects, such as Portrait mode.

Display your screen to others. During a FaceTime or other supported videoconferencing application session, it is simple to share a single app or multiple apps directly from the window. In the upper-left corner of the window, hover the cursor over the Mission Control key and select Share on FaceTime. Additionally, a video can be superimposed over a shared screen. Choose between large and tiny overlays. With your screen framed adjacent to you on a separate layer, the large overlay maintains the focus on you. In contrast, the small overlay renders you in a movable sphere above the shared screen. Select the Video symbol within the menu bar, then select Presenter Overlay size (large or small).

A user of the large Presenter Overlay in the course of a Zoom meeting.

Demonstrate what is available to you. By utilizing Desk View in conjunction with your MacBook Air and an iPhone, you cannot only display your face but also the content that is currently visible to you. To partake in a FaceTime call using Desk View, configure your iPhone as a webcam and then select Desk View in the FaceTime window's upper right corner on your Mac. If not, select Desk View from the menu bar by clicking the Video symbol . After aligning your workstation with the window using the controls, select Share Workstation View. To terminate Desk View sharing, select Close ⊗ from within the Desk View interface. Desk View is accessible on iPhone 11 and later models.

To transfer a FaceTime call or utilize an iPhone as a webcam for a Mac, the Continuity Camera feature must be enabled in the AirPlay & Handoff settings of an iPad or iPhone. Additionally, the same Apple ID must be used to sign in to all three devices: an iPhone, iPad, as well as MacBook Air. It is necessary to enable Bluetooth, WiFi, as well as Handoff on your iPhone, iPad, as well as Mac.

FaceTime can be used in groups. In a group call, you can communicate with up to 32 individuals. Generate an exclusive hyperlink for dissemination among a group. Select Link Creation. Transfer the hyperlink to the Clipboard or distribute it to your acquaintances via Messages or Mail. FaceTime conversations can now be joined via a link on devices other than Apple products.

A FaceTime window containing an invited group of users.

A FaceTime link can be appended to a Calendar event to postpone a call.

Respond to the discourse. Incorporate 3D effects that adorn the camera frame, such as pyrotechnics, hearts, debris, and more, into a reaction. Select a reaction by clicking the Video symbol  within the menu bar, followed by the menu next to Reactions. A reaction can also be expressed through the use of a and gesture.

Recognition of sign language and live captioning. FaceTime distinguishes sign language users by elevating their profile during group FaceTime conversations. FaceTime Live Captions present captions in real-time for the active speaker based on what is said.

Observe and listen in tandem. Utilize SharePlay on a Mac to listen and view together. Additionally screen sharing is possible during FaceTime calls. To begin, click the SharePlay icon.

Note: Participation in certain SharePlay-compatible applications requires a paid subscription. In some regions and countries, access to particular features and content is restricted.

Dial the telephone number. Mac users with an iPhone running iOS 8 or later can utilize FaceTime to make phone calls. Simply ensure that both your Mac and iPhone are equipped with the feature and are enrolled in using the identical Apple ID account (Initiate FaceTime on your Mac, navigate to FaceTime > Settings, and then choose "Calls from iPhone.")

Please be advised that to make or receive conversations on your Mac, both your iPhone as well as MacBook Air must be linked to the same Wi-Fi network as well as the internet.

**MAIL**

A single application is required to administer all of your email accounts with Mail. Compatible with the majority of widely used email platforms, including iCloud, Gmail, Yahoo Mail, as well as AOL Mail.

Establish email accounts. Experiencing fatigue from logging into multiple websites to access your email accounts? Configure Mail for each of your accounts to view all of your messages in a single location. Navigate to Mail > Add Account.

Organize your correspondence. Specify which messages should be displayed in your inbox. Mute excessively active email channels, block messages from particular senders by transferring them directly to the Trash, as well as unsubscribe from mailing lists through Mail. Additionally, you can filter the inbox to display only unread messages.

Remind me to send it at a later time. Prearrange the delivery of an email at the optimal moment. Next to the Send option, select the drop-down menu while composing a message. Customize a date and time by selecting one of the suggested intervals from the list or by selecting "Send Later." Additionally, you can specify a time and date to receive a reminder regarding an opened email that you failed to reply to. Control-click and select Remind Me from any email in the inbox. The selected time for the reminder will cause the message to reappear at the highest point of your inbox.

Undo submit. Simplify the process of unsending a recently sent email before it arrives in the recipient's inbox. Select Undo Send within 10 seconds of sending in Mail via the bottom of the sidebar. The amount of time you are given to unsend an email is also customizable. Proceed to Mail Preferences > Composing and select an option next to Undo Send Delay from the pop-up menu.

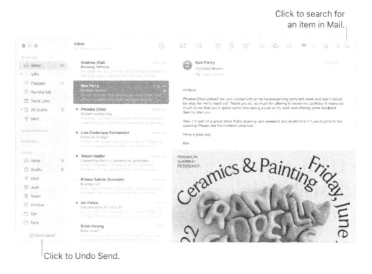

Click to search for an item in Mail.

Click to Undo Send.

A Mail window displaying the sidebar containing iCloud folders, Favourites, as well as Smart Mailboxes on the left, the array of messages adjacent to the sidebar, as well as the selected message's contents on the right.

Query Siri. For example, "Write Laura an email regarding the trip."

Locate the proper message. Enter your query into the search field to obtain recommendations for messages that most closely correspond to it. Mail includes an intelligent search feature that offers more precise results, detects typographical errors, and looks for synonyms of the entered search terms. While searching for email messages, intelligent search also provides a more comprehensive view of shared material along with other relevant information.

Safeguard your privacy. Privacy Protection safeguards against the disclosure of any data regarding one's email activity to email senders. It conceals your IP address when you enable it, preventing senders from correlating it with your other online activities or determining your location. Additionally, it hinders senders from ascertaining whether an individual has opened their email. Enable it by navigating to Mail Settings > Privacy and selecting Protect Mail Activity.

Avoid missing any emails. A notification shows up in the upper-right corner of the screen whenever you receive a new email, allowing you to rapidly preview incoming messages. (Avoid receiving notifications? To disable them, navigate to System Preferences and select Notifications from the sidebar. To configure your notification settings, navigate to Application Notifications on the right and select Mail.)

 **MESSAGES**

Messages make it simple to maintain communication, irrespective of the device being used. Manage group communications, pin favorites to the top, and view content shared by others with ease, among many other capabilities. iMessage allows you to transmit text messages to individuals who own an Apple Watch, Mac, iPhone, iPad, or iPod touch.

Alternatively, SMS/MMS can be used to send texts to others.

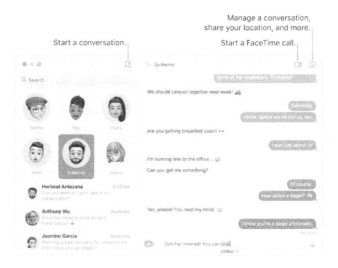

A Message window that provides instructions on initiating a FaceTime contact or conversation.

Messages are unlimited with iMessage. Upon logging in with your Apple ID, you can communicate with anyone who owns a Mac, iPhone, iPad, iPod touch, or Apple Watch indefinitely. This includes text, photos, Live Photos, video, and other media types. These gadgets receive encrypted messages from the Messages app via iMessage; the encrypted messages are displayed in blue bubbles within your conversations. Consult the Apple Support article Utilize Messages on your Mac for configuration instructions.

Provide MMS/SMS. You can send and receive messages via SMS and MMS on the Mac without using iMessage if your iPhone (running iOS 8.1 or later) is signed in to Messages with the same Apple

ID as your Mac. To enable Text Message Forwarding on your iPhone, navigate to Settings > Messages, touch Text Message Forwarding, and then select the name of the Mac you are using. An activation code will be displayed on your Mac if you are not utilizing two-factor authentication with your Apple ID. Once the code has been entered on the iPhone, select Allow. MMS and SMS messages appear in your conversations as green bubbles as well as are not encrypted.

Query Siri. Communicate with your mother as follows: "Please be advised that I will be arriving late."

Edit as well as unsend messages. You're able to unsend a recently sent message for up to two minutes after it has been sent or modify it up to five times within fifteen minutes of its initial transmission when using Messages for communication. Control-click any message that has been sent, then select Edit or Undo Send.

Designate a dialogue as unopened. You may designate an unread message for future reference when you have the opportunity to respond. In the messages list, control-click the read message, then select Mark as Unread.

Preserve preferred discussions at the forefront. By dragging your preferred conversations to the head of the messages display, you can pin them there. Tapbacks, input indicators, as well as new messages are displayed above a pinned conversation. In a group conversation, the most recent participants unanswered messages are displayed within the pinned conversation.

Oversee group discussions. Establish a group image consisting of a photo, Memoji, or emoji to facilitate group identification. You may direct a message to an individual within a group conversation by doing so via the person's name or by swiping right on any message. Additionally, you can provide an embedded reply to a query or statement made earlier in the conversation. While a conversation becomes excessively lively, it is possible to conceal conversation alerts. Click the Details icon ⓘ in the upper-right portion of the Messages window after selecting the conversation from the list to access the options for managing the conversation and setting group image. Select the "Notify me when my name is mentioned" checkbox under Messages > Settings General to be notified when your name is mentioned.

Enliven communications with humor. Animate conversations by providing replies containing stickers, Tapbacks, trending GIFs, or special effects such as balloons, billowing confetti, as well as more. You can synchronize stickers created on your iPhone with iCloud to have them accessible on your iPad, iPhone, as well as Mac. To insert a sticker into conversation, select Stickers from the Apps menu then select the one that most accurately reflects your disposition. Additionally, any sticker can be dropped and dragged to a particular message in the conversation. Select a Tapback, which could be a thumbs-up or thumbs-down, by clicking and holding a message. Click the Apps icon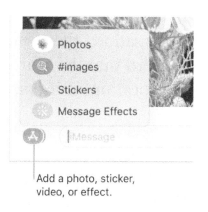, select #images or Message Effects, and then select the desired GIF or special effect. Additionally, be wary of handwritten messages, Digital Touch, and invisible ink that your peers may send you via their Apple Watch, iPhone, or iPad.

The Applications menu contains choices for displaying message effects, photographs, emoticons, and GIFs.

Develop an original Memoji. Create a customized Memoji by selecting your preferred hairstyle and color, skin tone and blemishes, facial features, as well as more. To set a customized Memoji as the background image for your Messages, navigate to Messages > Settings. Customize after clicking "Set up Name as well as Photo Sharing," followed by "Continue." After clicking the New Memoji icon, customize your appearance by clicking on each feature. Once complete, select Done to incorporate the Memoji into your collection of stickers. Open a conversation, select the Apps button , then the Stickers button, then the New Memoji button $+$, and then have fun devising additional Memojis to add to your collection.

Transmit an image, file, or video. Share files with ease by dragging them to Messages. Or locate and transmit videos and pictures from your Photos library with ease. Select Photos from the Apps menu within a conversation, then select a photo to insert. Enter a keyword into the search field, such as the name, date, or location of a person, to locate a particular image.

Simple image management. When an individual forwards you a collection of photographs, two to three of them are displayed as a collage that can be quickly inspected, while four or more are stacked. Swipe the stack with two fingertips to the left or right on a trackpad or Magic Mouse to view each image without opening it. To interact with a photo, remark to it, or add a Tapback, control-click on it. Select the Save Photo icon adjacent to an image to save it to Photos immediately. Right-clicking the heap twice will reveal every image within.

Locate the proper message. You can locate the desired message more rapidly by combining search filters to restrict your results. Peruse the results of a rapid search of your conversations by various criteria, including person and keyword, and by category, including photos, messages, and conversations.

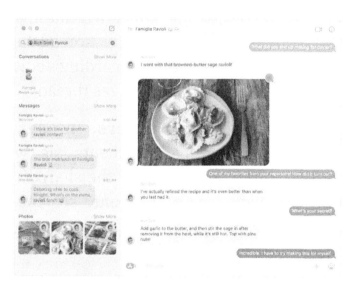

A window in Messages that demonstrates how to make use of the Shared with You search. Users' Contacts' content that is transmitted to them via Messages appears automatically in the corresponding app's Shared with You section, allowing them to access it at their convenience. Content that has been shared with you is accessible via the Apple TV app, Photos, Safari, Apple News, and Apple Podcasts. You can view the sender of shared content within the corresponding applications as well as with a single click, access the corresponding Messages conversation, allowing you to continue the dialogue while you enjoy the shared content.

To view every photo associated with a conversation, select the Details icon ⓘ.

Work together on endeavors. Invitations to collaborate on files, Keynote demonstrations,

Numbers spreadsheets, Pages documents, as well as Notes, among other things, are sendable. To initiate collaboration within the desired application, tap the Share icon, ensure Collaborate is selected, and then tap Messages. Upon selecting the group's name, all members of the thread are appended automatically as participants to the shared file, spreadsheet, or document. Activity updates regarding edits are displayed at the head of the Messages thread.

Display your display to others. In addition to opening folders, creating documents, as well as copying files to the desktop from the shared screen, you and a companion can also share screens. After selecting the Details switch ⓘ, proceed to select the Screen Share icon ▢.

Observe as well as listen in tandem. Join a SharePlay session on a Mac through Messages to jointly view and listen. Additionally, screen sharing is possible during FaceTime calls.

Note: Participation in certain SharePlay-compatible applications requires a paid subscription. In some regions as well as countries, access to particular content and features is restricted.

Implement a message filter with Focus Observe exclusively the desired messages throughout a specific Focus. To illustrate, for a Gaming Focus, simply observe discussions among acquaintances with whom you frequently engage in multiplayer games. After selecting Apple Menu > System Preferences, select Focus from the sidebar. Select a focus on the right, then select Add Filter⟩ under Focus Filters by clicking the right arrow.

 **FIND MY**

Use Find My to locate family, acquaintances, as well as Apple gadgets within the same application.

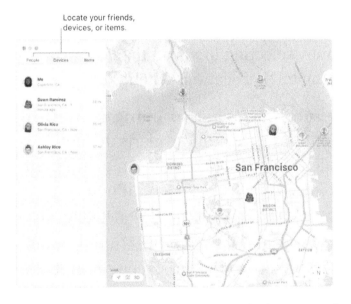

A Find My window featuring the People tab chosen on the left and a San Francisco map containing the coordinates of two acquaintances and yourself on the right.

It should be noted that the availability of Find My features may vary across regions and languages.

Locations can be shared with peers. Simply select Share My Location in the People list to inform family and friends of your current location. You may choose to share your live location indefinitely, for an hour, for a day, or an entire day. Additionally, you can request to follow an acquaintance to obtain detailed instructions about their location as well as view their location on a map.

Configure location notifications. Notify acquaintances automatically of your arrival and departure from a specified location. Configure notifications for the arrival and departure of you contacts. You can view all location-related notifications that your peers send you in a single location by selecting Me from the People list and then navigating to Notifications About You.

Notify me if I forget to bring something with me. Configure separation alerts to notify you that you've left the MacBook Air or a different gadget behind on your iPod touch, iPhone, or iPad. To configure separation alerts for a gadget, select Notify When Left Behind from the Info symbol ⓘ and afterward adhere to the on-screen prompts.

Protect a misplaced device. Protect and locate misplaced devices, such as your Mac, iPhone, or AirPods, using Find My. To locate a device on the map, select it from the Devices list by clicking on it Selecting the Info symbol ⓘ grants access to various functionalities, including the ability to remotely erase the gadget, designate it as lost to prevent unauthorized access to your private data, or play a sound to help you locate it.

A close-up of the MacBook Air's Info icon belonging to Danny.

Devices can be located even though they are inactive. When your gadget fails to connect to a Wi-Fi or cellular network, Find My uses Bluetooth signals from adjacent Apple devices to locate it. Under their encryption and anonymity, these signals assist in locating your misplaced device while safeguarding your privacy. Additionally, it is possible to locate a deleted device on iPads, iPhones, and iPod touch devices running iOS 15 or later, as well as Mac computers with macOS 12 or later.

Determine the location of a family member's gadget. If your family member is sharing the location of the gadget with you and you are a member of a Family Sharing group, you can use Find My to assist in locating the device.

Locate commonplace products. Attach an AirTag to an item such as your keychain so that you can locate it rapidly if you become disoriented. Register AirTags and compatible third-party products with your Apple ID using an iOS or iPadOS device. Click the Items pane in Find My to locate items on a Mac, and then select an item from the list to observe its coordinates on the map. You can verify the item's most recent whereabouts and be notified when it is located again if it cannot be located. Additionally, Lost Mode can be activated for items that contain both a message and a phone number.

FREEFORM

Utilize Freeform to facilitate collaboration and idea organization. After establishing a board, you may include text, media, files, and more. Monitor and collaborate on adjustments in real time.

Freeform is compatible with macOS Ventura 13.1 and newer.

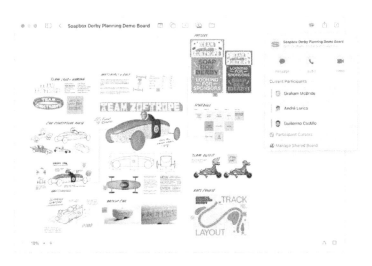

A Freeform board containing instances of an ideation session and the collaboration option in an active state.

Establish a board. To create a new board, select the New Board icon from the toolbar. Boards are automatically stored. Enter a name for a board by selecting Untitled from the title bar's upper-left corner.

Boards are synchronized across all devices. To synchronize your boards, enable Freeform in the iCloud Preferences. Freeform is compatible with iPadOS 16.2 and iOS 16.2.

Include media files, text, and more. Insert text, sticky notes, images, URLs, and files into your board using the toolbar. You can also drag items from other applications to your board.

Establish a structure for your board. Item alignment, resizing, grouping, and movement are all possible on your board. Additionally, alignment cues and a grid view of your board are both options that can assist you in positioning items.

Produce a diagram. A diagram can be constructed by utilizing various elements such as shapes, lines, and other components. Select View, followed by Display Connectors. Drag an arrow after inserting any form of element—text, shapes, or post-it notes—to insert a connector line.

Work together in Freeform. You can either copy and share the link or send a request to collaborate on a board via Messages or Mail. Select Collaborate from the toolbar's Share option, then choose Messages, Mail, or Copy Link. All individuals participating in the conversation are extended invitations to the board via Messages.

The output is a PDF file. A PDF file can be generated from a Freeform board export. Select File > PDF Export.

SHORTCUTS

The Shortcuts application enables the execution of multi-step processes with a single tap or by utilizing Siri. Create shortcuts to transfer text between applications, obtain directions to the next event within your calendar, as well as more. To execute multiple stages of a task, select pre-made shortcuts from the Shortcuts Gallery or create your own using various applications.

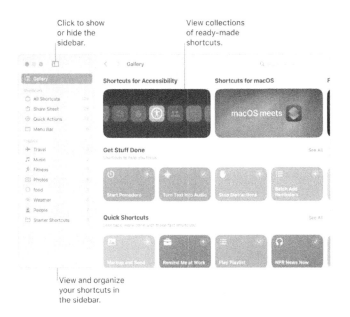

Click to show or hide the sidebar.

View collections of ready-made shortcuts.

View and organize your shortcuts in the sidebar.

A gallery of potentialities. Search the Gallery for shortcuts or peruse them. A variety of frequent duties are represented by starter shortcuts that are organized into collections. In the My Shortcuts section of the Gallery sidebar, both the shortcuts that you generate and any pre-made shortcuts that you modify are displayed. To toggle the Gallery sidebar's visibility, select the Sidebar icon.

Develop personal shortcuts. To achieve the desired result, generate a new shortcut and then transfer actions from the list of actions on the right to the shortcut editor on the left. A shortcut is composed of actions, which are analogous to the phases in a task. Select from an extensive array of options, including importing the current URL from Safari, generating a folder, or retrieving the most recent photo from the Photos application. Also possible are actions that execute a script and perform calculations, rounding a number, or activating aircraft mode. Additionally, Shortcuts offers "next action" recommendations to aid in the completion of the shortcut.

Your shortcuts as shortcuts. Siri's execution of shortcut is the most efficient method for accomplishing a task. Additionally, shortcuts can be added to the Services Menu and the Finder. Click Shortcut Details ⓘ after performing a double-click on a shortcut, and then select Options under Use a Quick Action.

Query Siri. Propose the following: "Text the final image."

Share and synchronize settings. Using the same Apple ID across all of your devices will cause you shortcuts to be displayed on each one. Any changes you save on one device are reflected automatically on all of your other gadgets. Additionally, one can receive shortcuts that have been shared by another user. To share an item, double-click the shortcut, then select the desired sharing method. Additionally, auxiliary shortcuts for common operations can be added to the Share Sheet.

 iMOVIE

With a few simple taps, iMovie enables you to transform your videos into stunning films as well as Hollywood-style trailers that you can share.

Acquire a video. Video can be imported from a camera, an iPhone, iPad, or iPod touch, or from media assets that are already present on a Mac. An event as well as a library are generated for you by iMovie.

An iMovie window containing the controls for sharing the movie, trailer, or film segment, rectifying as well as altering colors, as well as viewing projects.

Capture video using the integrated camera. Record video using the FaceTime HD camera on the Mac as well as incorporate it into your project. To begin and end recording, select an event from the sidebar, select Import within the toolbar, choose FaceTime HD Camera, and afterward select the Record icon.

Create trailers in the manner of Hollywood. Construct astute promos that feature animated visuals and uplifting musical scores. Simply incorporate images and videos while personalizing the credits. Click the New icon✛, then select a template within the Trailer window, before clicking Create to begin. In the Outline tab, include the performers and credits; in the Storyboard tab, include your videos and pictures.

Click Play to preview the trailer.

The trailer screen for iMovie displays the Play icon.

Although video captured with a handheld device may appear unsteady, it is possible to stabilize the footage for a more fluid viewing experience. After selecting the film in the timeline, pick Stabilization, followed by Stabilize Shaky Video🎥.

TV

Stream any movie or television program using the Apple TV app. Subscribing to channels, purchasing or renting movies and television programs, and continuing to view from any of your gadgets is possible.

Commence your usage of Watch Now. Peruse a curated feed of suggestions in Watch Now, which is informed by the channels to which you have subscribed as well as the movies or television programs that you have previously viewed.

Continue to observe Up Next. You'll discover movies and television programs you're currently viewing and those you've added to your queue in Up

Next. To include a new television program or film in Up Next, select the Add to Up Next icon.

Learn more about Films, Television Shows, and Children. To locate a particular item, select Movies, TV Shows, or Kids from the menu bar and then navigate by genre.

Subscribe, rent, or purchase. After discovering a desired film or television program, you have the option of purchasing or renting it. Through Family Sharing, channels to which you have subscribed are accessible on all devices and can be utilized by up to six family members.

Observe the content that your peers are sharing. When you receive programs and films from family and friends via the Messages application, you have the flexibility to view them at your convenience. Simply search for them in a new section of Watch Now titled Shared With You within the Apple TV app. Content is only displayed in Shared with You if the sender is a contact of yours.

Attend the show together. FaceTime enables you to establish connections with your friends, while SharePlay enables you to view a movie or television program with family as well as friends—and even exchange remarks in Messages whilst you watch Select the Play icon after hovering the cursor over any item in the TV application to begin viewing While conversing with pals on your iPhone, you can view content on your Mac. Additionally, intelligent intensity adjusts the audio automatically so that everyone can hear one another during raucous situations.

It is necessary to have iPadOS 15.4 or later on the iPad as well as macOS 12.3 or later on your Mac to utilize SharePlay. Some SharePlay-compatible applications demand a paid subscription to function. In some regions and countries, access to particular features and content is restricted.

Select an item from your library. To view a genre-organized list of all the movies and television programs you've purchased or downloaded, select Library. To begin viewing, simply select the film or television program.

 **MAPS**

Locate objects and obtain directions by utilizing a satellite image or a map. Apple has curated guides that provide suggestions for the top attractions in a given city. A location can be force-clicked to place a mark there.

Investigate in depth. To facilitate exploration, maps provide additional information such as elevation, natural features, landmarks, and more. View city experiences on a Mac powered by Apple silicon include landmarks, structures, and foliage among other details.

Make preparations for your route. Utilize the updated road map to determine your route, monitor traffic conditions, and view road specifics such as bus and turn lanes. Automatically access route plans containing multiple locations on your iPhone, or expeditiously communicate directions to a companion through Messages.

Locate and store preferred items. Identify the desired information and refine the outcomes. Gain access to vital details by selecting a location, such as the operating hours of a business or the availability of delivery at a restaurant. The locations that you frequent most frequently can be saved as favorites.

A San Francisco map that depicts a museum. A portal containing information displays vital details about the enterprise.

Query Siri. Utilize the phrase "Find coffee near me

Explore unfamiliar locales with the aid of guides. To facilitate the exploration, dining, and shopping in renowned global destinations, Maps provides curated guides authored by reputable brands as well as partners. These guides are downloadable as well as will be updated as new locations are introduced.

Produce customized instructions. You can publish personalized guides for your preferred destinations and distribute them to your loved ones. To generate a guide, hover over My Guides in the top sidebar, select the Add symbol⊕ on the right, and then control-click the newly created guide to access its settings.

Analyze in 3D. By activating the Look Around binoculars symbol👓, users can navigate interactively through the streets of select cities while experiencing a three-dimensional exploration. The Earth's natural grandeur can be experienced through the interactive 3D Globe on a Mac equipped with Apple silicon.

For indoor maps of significant locations. Orient yourself within specific airports and retail centers. Simply magnify the image to locate nearby dining establishments, restrooms, and gathering spots with friends at the mall, as well as additional information.

A Maps window demonstrating how to locate your current location on the map, how to obtain directions by selecting a destination within the sidebar, and how to access and dismiss the sidebar.

Travel there employing public transportation. For select cities, Maps provides Nearby Transit information, including imminent departures in your vicinity. Select an intended location from the sidebar, and subsequently tap the Transit symbol to obtain estimated travel time, suggested routes, and transit fares. Favorite transit lines can be pinned to the top so that they always appear when they are nearby.

Electric vehicle journey planning simplified. When you link your electric vehicle to your iOS device, Maps not only displays the locations of charging stations but also computes your estimated time of arrival to account for charging periods.

Develop a cycling route plan. Mapping provides essential information for organizing a bicycle excursion, including but not limited to altitude, traffic conditions, as well as the presence of precipitous inclines. Once your itinerary is finalized, you can transfer it to your iPhone.

Receive real-time ETA notifications. When family and acquaintances provide you with their ETA, Maps can display their current location along the route.

Certain Maps functionalities are not accessible in every country or region.

Tip: To observe the nature of traffic, select Show Traffic from the View menu within the menu bar.

VOICE MEMOS

Using Voice Memos to record personal reminders, class lectures, interviews, or even song ideas is more convenient than ever. iCloud enables users to conveniently access voice recordings captured on their iPhone directly from their MacBook Air.

A Voice Memos interface displays an active recording.

Utilize your MacBook Air to record. To cease recording, click Done after selecting the Record option ●. Renaming a recording would facilitate its identification. After selecting the default name, input a new one. To have your recording played back, select the Play icon ▶.

Voice recordings are accessible from any device. By logging in with the same Apple ID across all of your gadgets, your voice memos become accessible. Specifically, recordings that were created on your iPhone or iPad can be accessed directly from your Mac.

Implement folder. Establishing folders will assist you in organizing your Voice Memos. Select the Sidebar button ⊟ followed by the New Folder icon located at the bottom of the sidebar to create a new folder. After entering the folder's name, select the Save button. While dragging the recording to the olster, hold down the Option key to add the recording to the folder.

Mark recordings as Favorites.

00:57.66

Create new folders to organize your recordings.

The Voice Memos interface includes buttons for creating new folders and marking recordings as favorites.

Indicate a track as a favorite. Choose a recording, and finally choose the Favourite icon♡ in the toolbar to ensure that the recording is easily accessible in the future. To display your favorites, select the Sidebar link⌷.

Ignore silence. Avoid pausing in the audio. Enable Skip Silence by clicking the Playback Settings icon at the highest point of the Voice Memos window.

Accelerate the playback rate. Adjust the tempo of your audio. Dragging the slider to the left or right after clicking the Playback Settings icon at the highest point of the Voice Memos window is possible.

Improving a recording. Reducing room reverberation and background noise will enhance the

181

sound quality of your Voice Memos. Enable Enhance Recording by clicking the Playback Settings icon located at the highest point within the Voice Memos window.

NOTES

One can best record brief thoughts or store more extensive notes that include images, web links checklists, and more in Notes. Collaboration functionalities, such as activity view, mentions, a well as shared notes as well as folders, facilitat working with others and ensure that you are alway aware of the latest developments in your note Additionally, one may employ Tags to enhanc organization or utilize Smart Folders to automaticall categorize notes according to specific criteria, such a the presence of checklists or attachments, the date c creation or modification, and other relevant factor; Moreover, iCloud simplifies the process c synchronizing every one of your gadgets, ensurin that your notes are consistently accessible on an gadget to which you have logged in with your Appl ID.

Query Siri. Pronounce the following: "Generate fresh note."

Share notes, add content, and secure then Add checklists, photographs, videos, illustration tables, and URLs to your notes with ease using th

Notes toolbar. To format text, such as by adding a list, creating a heading, or formatting text as a block quote, select the Font icon AA. To secure your note with the MacBook Air's logon password or to generate a unique password, select the Lock icon🔒. To distribute a note via Mail, Messages, Reminders, or AirDrop, select Send Copy from the Share menu⬆️, then select the desired sharing method.

The toolbar for taking notes includes icons for the following: text format, checklist, table, link, photos/media, secure, share, and send a copy.

Discuss in concert a note. You may copy and distribute the link or send an invitation to collaborate via Messages or Mail on a note. From the Collaborate menu that appears after clicking the Share icon⬆️ in the toolbar, select Messages, Mail, or Copy Link. When the link is shared in Messages, all participants in the thread are included in the list automatically. After inviting others to participate, selecting the Collaborate icon👥 enables you to monitor activity and manage collaboration.

Linking to an additional note inside an existing note.

Link to additional annotations. To establish a hyperlink to an additional note, enter ">>" into a note, and then select the desired note from the resulting list. If the desired note is not visible in the list, begin entering its title until it does. To generate a hyperlink to a newly added note, enter the note's title followed by the Create Note "[note title]" button. A new entry is appended to the list of notes.

Include tags. To classify and arrange the contents of your note, employ keywords throughout its body. Enter the tag text followed by the # symbol. By displaying your tags within the sidebar, you can easily navigate to notes that contain a particular tag or tags (e.g., #cooking or #vacation). Using the same categories, custom smart folders instantly compile notes in one location.

A memo is opened in Pages. Simply import your notes into Pages without the need for manual copying and pasting. Select Open in Pages after clicking the Share icon⬆ on the note. Any changes made in Pages or Notes after opening a note in Pages are version-specific.

Employ mentions. By including mentions (e.g., @Leslie followed by a name), you can establish direct communication with your collaborators in a social context or during a project. Upon receiving notification that they have been referenced in a note, they will be able to immediately engage in the discussion.

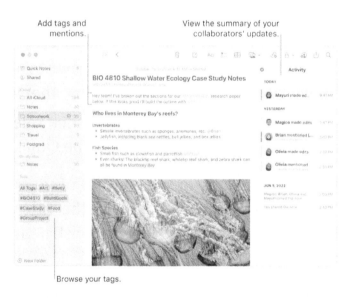

Add tags and mentions.

View the summary of your collaborators' updates.

Browse your tags.

A Notes window within the Gallery view that includes a sidebar with a callout to categories. The primary note includes both a mention and a callout to a tag. An activity list featuring a callout to access a summary of the updates is displayed on the right.

View the activity summary of a note. Access current information regarding the contributors to a collaborative note by utilizing the Activity view located to the right of the Notes window. To access editor callouts that display highlighted modifications as well as the date and time of the note's revision, swipe right on the note text.

Create a Quick Note from any location. You can create notes from any application or website on the Mac using Quick Note, which will then appear within the Quick Notes section of the Sidebar.

To generate a Quick Note, position the cursor in the lower-right portion of the display, which serves as the default Hot portion for Quick Note. Or, utilize the -Q keyboard shortcut⊕.

Note: To designate a different Hot Corner to a Quick Note, navigate to System Settings via the System Settings symbol ◎ > Desktop & Dock, then select Hot Corners. Select the desired corner for the Quick Note.

Modify the dimensions or orientation of your Quick Note (drag a corner to resize it, or the title bar to reposition it) to prevent it from obstructing the current view.

Personalize the interface. Control-clicking any location within the toolbar will reveal the Customize Toolbar window. Simply drag and drop your preferred objects into the toolbar to activate them.

Drag your favorite items into the toolbar.

...or drag the default set into the toolbar.

Done

A Notes window displaying the available options for customizing the toolbar.

 MUSIC

Organizing and listening to your iTunes Store purchases, albums, as well as songs in your library and the Apple Music catalog (which provides on-demand access to millions of tunes) is a breeze with the Apple Music app. To view upcoming, previously played, and currently playing lyrics, click. Utilize the iTunes Store to acquire the music you desire.

You have it in your library. Your iTunes Store purchases, items added from the Apple Music catalog, as well as music in your library are all readily observable and playable. Artists, albums, songs, or recently Added can be used to filter your content.

Exploration of the finest Apple Music. To view fresh and exclusive releases from Apple Music, a paid monthly music streaming service, select Browse from the sidebar. Stream and download over fifty million songs without interruption, and peruse an extensive library of recordings to locate the ideal arrangement for any occasion. To receive notifications regarding

187

new music as well as suggestions from other artists that you may find appealing, it is now possible to follow your preferred artists.

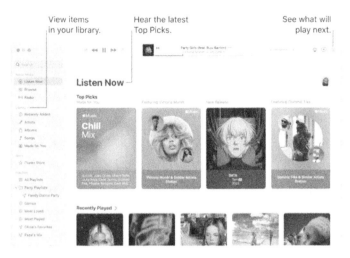

Join and sing along. When accessible, clicking in the toolbar will reveal a panel containing the lyric of the current song.

Attend to it. To tune in to Apple Music 1 live or an episode from the Apple Music family of shows, selec Radio from the sidebar. Investigate the assortment c stations designed for virtually every musical genre.

Query Siri. State something along the lines of "Ad this song to my library."

Sync effortlessly. Sync your music directly withi the Apple Music application. Upon connecting device, it becomes visible in the Finder's sideba Simply transfer the desired content onto your devic Additionally, device backups and restores a possible via the Finder.

Listen in unison. Utilize SharePlay to listen to music with up to 32 peers in real time. Commence by convening the group via FaceTime, and subsequently proceed by clicking. Click the Play icon after hovering the cursor over a song or album within the Music application to begin listening. All users are simultaneously exposed to the same music and are granted access to the shared playback controls, as well as being able to rearrange or add tracks to the shared music queue. Additionally, intelligent intensity adjusts the audio automatically so that everyone can hear one another even during raucous passages.

It is necessary to have iPadOS 15.4 or later on your iPad as well as macOS 12.3 or later on your Mac to utilize SharePlay. Some SharePlay-compatible applications demand a paid subscription to function. In some regions and countries, access to particular features and content is restricted.

Obtain it from the App Store. To acquire ownership of your music, select iTunes Store from the sidebar. (To view the iTunes Store within the sidebar, navigate to Music > Settings > General > Show iTunes Store.)

When screen space is at a premium, consider the following: By navigating to MiniPlayer, a small movable window will appear, allowing you to manipulate and listen to music on your Mac while performing other tasks. You can also move this window with your mouse. To initiate MiniPlayer, navigate to Window > MiniPlayer.

Podcasts that are currently being listened to are retained in Listen Now under Apple ID, irrespective of the device on which the listening originated.

Query Siri. Say something along the lines of "Keep the previous podcast playing" or "Subscribe to this podcast."

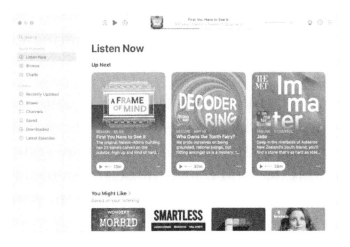

Explore fresh podcasts. Listen Now provides recommendations for new podcasts based on topics and shows, while Top Charts lists the most popular programs. Subscribe to the podcast or save an episode to your library if you find one that you enjoy. You can view the recommendations your peers make in Shared with You and receive recommendations for similar programs as well as topics based on your preferences.

Conveyed to You. The episodes of podcasts that are shared with you via Messages from contacts within your Contacts have been added to the Shared with You section of Listen Now within Apple Podcasts.

Episodes can be added to a library. Click ╋ to add an individual episode to your library. To subscribe to an entire podcast and receive new episodes, simply select Subscribe. Select ⬇ to obtain a podcast for listening offline.

Navigate by guest or host. When you search for a particular subject or individual, outcomes may include appearances on their programs, as well as appearances on shows where they are discussed or mentioned.

Maintain a follow for your favorites. By adding a program to your favorites via the Follow button, you are never missing a new episode. Visit your library's Recently Updated section to discover recent additions.

Organize thoughts using Quick Note. Interested in bookmarking a podcast for your upcoming road vacation or to synchronize with while exercising? Simply generate a Quick Note to retain the information for future reference. Fn-Q or a designated hot corner in Podcasts can be utilized to create a quick note as well as save the podcast link.

Later, the Quick Note will be accessible via the Notes application's sidebar.

AirPlay can be utilized to stream music, podcasts, or radio through an external speaker. Tap Screen Mirroring from the Control Centre icon in the menu bar, followed by the selection of an available speaker.